To Dad, for inspiring me to imagine great things;
To Mom, for teaching me to create with compassion;
To my Mother-In-Law, for keeping me grounded in love;
And to my wife, for giving me wings to follow my dreams.

From Paper
To Pixels

Your Guide to the
Digital Sheet Music Revolution

Hugh Sung

KaSu Press

From Paper to Pixels

From Paper to Pixels: Your Guide to the Digital Sheet Music
Revolution
By Hugh Sung
Published by KaSu Press
P.O. Box 3359
Nederland, Colorado 80466
Cover Art and graphics by Hugh Sung

Edited by James Townsend
iCloud, iPad, iPad Mini, iPhone, iPod, iPot Touch, iTunes, Mac, and
MacBook are trademarks of Apple, Inc.
Android and Google Drive are trademarks of Google Inc.
SkyDrive, Surface, Windows, and Windows Vista are trademarks of
Microsoft, Inc.
Kindle is a trademark of Amazon.com, Inc.
Samsung and Galaxy Tab are trademarks of Samsung Electronics Co.,
Ltd.
Dropbox is a trademark of Dropbox, Inc.
AirTurn is a trademark of AirTurn, Inc.
All products and software programs mentioned are trademarks of their
respective manufacturers and developers.

ISBN: 0-9896397-0-3
ISBN-13: 978-0-9896397-0-5

Printed in the United States of America
2013 - First KaSu Press Edition

How to Use This Book

While I would be thrilled if you read this book from cover to cover, the truth of the matter is that you might only find some portions relevant to your musical needs. If you're a classical musician, you probably have no clue what a tab sheet is. Likewise, if you primarily read lead sheets, then you probably don't really have an interest in music notation software. Nevertheless, you're bound to find something helpful within the pages of this guide, so I encourage you to peruse the table of contents and jump to the sections that are most relevant to your needs. You won't hurt my feelings, I promise!

Throughout this book, I'm going to be referring to a LOT of websites. Long strings of words that are underlined indicate the addresses of websites, such as: www.frompapertopixels.com

Now, I don't mean to rub this point in so early in this book, but one obvious disadvantage of paper books is the fact that you can't tap any of the underlined website addresses ("links" in web-speak) on the page and see a window magically pop up taking you to any of the websites. But if you have one of those fancy-dancy smartphones, like an iPhone or an Android phone, or even an iPod Touch with a camera in back, the good news is that you can use these handheld wonders to open up these websites much easier than having to type in colons and dashes and the gobblety gook letters that make up a website's address.

You're going to see a number of funny looking boxes with weird patterns inside, kind of like this one:

No, no, my printer isn't coughing up ink in some Emmy-award-grasping death scene - these boxes are called QR Codes ("QR" stands for "Quick Response"). You'll need to install a QR reader app in your smartphone or i-Device with a camera. Just do a search for "QR Reader" in your device's app store, or if you really love to type in cryptographic web addresses, here are some manual links to challenge your hand-eye coordination:

QR Reader for iPhone:
https://itunes.apple.com/us/app/qr-reader-for-iphone/id368494609?mt=8

QR Barcode Scanner for Android:
https://play.google.com/store/apps/details?id=appinventor.ai_progetto2003.SCAN&hl=en

Once you have a QR reading app on your device, fire it up, then follow the instructions -- normally you'll be asked to hover your smartphone or i-Device over the desired QR code box until your camera can focus in on it and auto-magically recognize what it's saying. In a few seconds, the website embedded in the QR code should pop up on your smartphone or i-Device. Nifty, eh?

If you don't have any of these types of phones that can install a QR reader app, don't despair. Just head on over to your computer and use your web browser of choice to go to www.frompapertopixels.com to get the latest and greatest content that will supplement this book. Videos! Tutorials! Pictures! Vibrant sounds! Content errata and updates! Need I say more?

Thank you for holding this book in your hand. I hope you find this to be a helpful and entertaining resource. If you have any questions or comments, feel free to email me at hugh@airturn.com.

Contents

11   **Chapter One**
From Paper to Pixels

16   **Chapter Two**
Ten Reason Why Pixels Are Better Than Paper

21   **Chapter Three**
A Short History of Digital Sheet-Music Readers

34   **Chapter Four**
What Do I Need to Get Started Reading Sheet Music
Digitally?

39   **Chapter Five**
The 5th C: The Art of Converting Paper to PDFs

53   **Chapter Six**
Transferring Converted Music to an iPad Using
Email

61   **Chapter Seven**
Transferring Converted Music to an iPad Using
Dropbox

71   **Chapter Eight**
Transferring Converted Music to an iPad using
iTunes

82   **Chapter Nine**
Transferring Digital Sheet Music to an Android
Tablet
– 84   Transferring Files to an Android Tablet
Using Email

– 93   Downloading PDF Files from Dropbox
– 98   Transferring Files to an Android Tablet Using a USB Cable
– 102   Transferring Files to An Android Tablet Using a USB Thumb Drive

103   **Chapter Ten**
My four-C Setup as a Digital Sheet-Music Musician

115   **Chapter Eleven**
Steve Hoover: Multi-Musician and His Four-C Digital Sheet-Music Setup

120   **Chapter Twelve**
Bob Bell: A Better Pager Turner for Organists

126   **Chapter Thirteen**
Sharyn Byer: A Forward-Looking Flutist

130   **Chapter Fourteen**
Caleb Overstreet: How to Conduct a Digital Revolution

134   **Chapter Fifteen**
Janette McIntyre: Computerized Cruise-Ship Cocktail Pianist

137   **Chapter Sixteen**
How to Select the Perfect Computer for Reading Digital Sheet Music, Part 1

140   **Chapter Seventeen**
Selecting the Perfect Computer for Reading Your Sheet Music: Three Key Questions

Contents

145 Chapter Eighteen
Selecting the Perfect Computer for Reading Sheet
Music: Mobile & Stationary Options
– 146 Mobile Computers
– 148 Stationary Computers
– 150 Hybrid Options
– 153 Screen Aspect Ratios

155 Chapter Nineteen
Finding the Perfect Digital Sheet-Music Reader, Part
1: Giants

161 Chapter 20
Finding the Perfect Digital Sheet-Music Reader, Part
2: Rainbows

164 Chapter Twenty-One
Finding the Perfect Digital Sheet-Music Reader, Part
3: Crystal Balls

173 Chapter Twenty-Two
Content, Part 1: An Overview of Digital Sheet-Music
Resources

177 Chapter Twenty-Three
Content, Part 2: Apps for Reading Paper Sheet-
Music Sources
– 179 PDF Apps/Programs
– 180 iPad Apps for Reading PDFs
– 186 Mac/PC Apps for Reading PDFs
– 187 Android Apps for Reading PDFs

190   Chapter Twenty-Four
Content, Part 3: Set Lists
– 202   The Evil Megalomaniacal Set-List Manager

204   Chapter Twenty-Five
Content, Part 4: On Overview of Internet Sheet-Music Sources

207   Chapter Twenty-Six
Content, Part Five: Commercial PDF Sheet-Music Resources

210   Chapter Twenty-Seven
Content, Part 6: Proprietary Sheet-Music Sites and Apps

215   Chapter Twenty-Eight
Content, Part 7: Free Sheet-Music Sites – Classical Resources
– 217   Classical/Public Domain Sites
– 219   Scholarly Editions

221   Chapter Twenty-Nine
Content, Part 8: Free Text-Based Sheet-Music Sites
– 226   Lyrics-Only Websites
– 228   Chords-Only Websites
– 229   Tabs Websites

231   Chapter Thirty
Content, Part 9: Text-Based Sheet-Music Apps
– 233   IOS Reader Apps
– 235   Android Text-Reader Apps

Contents

237   **Chapter Thirty-One**
So You Wanna Be a Beatle?

241   **Chapter Thirty-Two**
Cocktail Napkins, Canadians, and Chordpro
– 244   Text Music Styles
    – 244   Two-Line Style
    – 245   Rise-Up Style
    – 246   Chordpro Style
– 249   Chordpro Websites
– 250   Chordpro Programs for Mac and PC
– 254   Chordpro Apps for Tablets

255   **Chapter Thirty-Three**
Creating Musical Notation Content
– 256   Note-By-Note Input
– 259   Online Music Notation
– 265   Free-Play Notation
– 269   MIDI Hardware
– 278   MIDI Interfaces for Acoustic Instruments

281   **Chapter Thirty-Four**
Containers: Transforming a Digital Reader Into a
Music Stand
– 284   Tablet Mounts
– 297   Smartphone Mounts
– 299   Laptop Stands

301   **Chapter Thirty-Five**
Controllers: Expanding Ways to Work With your
Computer
– 302   A Page-Turner's Tale
– 319   Sleight of Palm: Pens for Tablets
– 325   Drawing Tablets for Mac and PC Computers

326 **Chapter Thirty-Six**
    Conclusion: It's Never Too Late

331 **Appendix A**
    How to Create Big-Note Music Using a Mac
339 **Appendix B**
    How to Create Big-Note Music Using a PC
352 **Appendix C**
    Big-Note Beta
356 **Appendix D**
    Pre-Performance Checklist
362 **Acknowledgements**
364 **About the Author**

CHAPTER ONE

From Paper to Pixels

If you are a musician who uses sheet music, then no doubt you've either experienced one of these painful situations yourself, or at least can shake your head in some pretense of sympathy (and yes, these all actually happened to me):

– I'm running through the airport in a mad, mad dash to catch a connecting flight. The bag slung over my shoulder holds about 50 pounds of sheet music, and I am having visions of being on the Inquisitor's rack, my shoulder slowly dislocating. I am dangerously close to blurting out, "I confess!"

– Speeding on the New Jersey Turnpike from Philadelphia to an important audition in New York City, I realize with horror at the halfway point that I forgot to pack the music I needed to accompany my client, a talented young clarinetist. There's not enough time to drive back home to find the music, and there's no point in continuing the drive to New York. I have ruined his audition and kicked my professional reputation into the gutter.

– A week before violin auditions, I'm at the library trying to collect all the music for the pieces the applicants are preparing. One is an obscure Russian concerto that – lo and not behold – is nowhere to be found in the library shelves. Or the local music store. I'm told that, given the byzantine Russian export laws at the time, it would take months before a copy of that piece could be tracked down and delivered. I pray the applicant is struck with an incapacitating pestilence.

– I've been invited to perform one of the piano parts in the wickedly difficult Bartok Sonata for Two Pianos and Percussion. With the potential for an ensemble train wreck written on every page of music, and given my general distrust of the reading skills of page-turners, I want to handle the page turns myself. But the pianist who invited me says that she doesn't want to be "shown up" by being the only one having to rely on a page-turner, so right before the performance she insists that I use one of her student page-turners. I reluctantly agree. I give the young Asian student with dubious English comprehension strict instructions NOT to turn any pages until I signal with a clear head nod. She nods nervously. Bad sign. We get to the middle of the first movement, and I'm reading the middle of the left page, hands flailing on the piano and concentrating on maintaining the tight musical ensemble. Suddenly, without warning, the page-turner bolts upright and turns the page – *a FULL page too soon*! I'm in shock, and the ensuing train wreck is ugly. From that moment, I swear my eternal hatred for human page-turners.

For the vast majority of musicians, dealing with heavy binders, misplaced scores, shipping delays, and illiterate page-turners is a normal part of the self-flagellation we deem necessary in the service of our beloved art. We devote countless hours of blood, sweat and tears to the daily practice and mastery of an instrument, while we consider the hassles of paper scores to be just another necessary evil, an ancient curse, perhaps, by an agent of the Devil upon some hapless lute or sackbut player of old.

But what if it were possible to be free of paper? What if we didn't have to deal with the clutter, bulk, weight and other limitations of physical space that paper sheet music requires? And what if, just as mechanical typewriters have given way to Macs and PCs (like Salieri symphonies, which have been eclipsed by Mozart's genius), there were digital ways of working with sheet music that actually are *better* than physical paper? Blasphemy, or simply outsmarting the Devil?

Either way, I confess: Several years after the incidents I describe above, I became, in essence, a "paperless pianist." My *entire library of 6,000 scores* is digitally contained in a sleek, 1.2-lb. mobile computer called an iPad.

Here's a peek into my brave new world:

– During a local concerto competition, I run into a flustered pianist who is apologizing to the violinist he was going to accompany that he has forgotten to bring his music (Ah, how painfully familiar that sounds!). I ask him which concerto he is missing, pull up my computer, and within seconds I have the missing piano part. I offer to either send the part to a printer, or to let him borrow my computer to read the music digitally. He looks at me like I've grown a second head.

– I'm finishing a tour with a flutist when we get a last-minute invitation to appear on a popular TV show. I have three days to put together an entirely different program than what we had just performed, including a request to transcribe some pop songs from MP3 audio files (the sheet music didn't exist). I transcribe and arrange the music digitally, and download the other pieces for the program from the Internet directly into my computer. Who needs paper or printer?

– A young violinist approaches me with a fiendishly difficult piece for violin and piano that is required for a major international competition. Given the difficulty of the piece, I recommend that he use a computer to read his music and a hands-free, page-turning pedal to turn his pages. That enables him to not only mark up his score in bright colors and highlights, but also to be able to see the full score as opposed to just his solo part, so that he has a complete view of both his and the pianist's parts. During the competition, all the other competitors are unfurling rows of their paper music across multiple music stands. My guy needs only one stand to hold his computer, and his page-turning pedal on the floor. He goes on to win the competition, including a special recognition of "best performance" for that piece. Yes!

Do you have a nostalgic devotion to your stacks of coffee-stained, curled, yellowed and smudged sheet music? Are you convinced that the scent of mildew it exudes somehow contains magic that makes you a better musician? Let me posit something that will revolutionize your world, if you let it:

Becoming a paperless musician will lead to faster, more effective learning and performance of music. It is physically more convenient, and will actually give you the tools to become a vastly better musician. To boot, it is a great way to be more environmentally friendly.

"But wait!" you say, clutching your 20-lb. fake book to your chest. "You mean I will have to give up my scores, binders, lyric sheets, chord charts ... and the ratty old briefcase I carry them around in?"

Perish the thought! Once you learn how simple it is to transform all that stuff into pixels, and how much more you'll be able to do with it, you can keep all your relics in the nearest closet, pull them out and sniff over them whenever you feel like things are moving too fast (You can put them right next to the cassette tapes you haven't been able to bear to part with). And you can walk into your gigs carrying your old briefcase, savoring the moment when you pull out your shiny iPad or tablet and set it on the music stand, and hear the sound of jaws hitting the floor all around you.

"But," you say, "I'm daunted by technology!" Not to fear. In this book, I will make your transition from paper to pixels easy and painless. You're going to be amazed at how quickly you'll discover the fantastic possibilities inherent in going digital. Together, we'll explore what it means, why it offers the best solutions for all types of musicians (even those who just need to remember the lyrics or edit the song list), and I'll walk you through everything ... gently.

Onward, my fellow musicians! The digital sheet-music revolution is at hand!

CHAPTER TWO

Ten Reasons Why Pixels Are Better Than Paper

Ok, just in case I didn't convince you in the introduction why you need to join the digital sheet-music revolution, here's more.

What the heck is a pixel?

For my musician friends who are still dragging their consciousness (and their sheet music) out of the last century (or even the 1800s), pixels are the smallest dots on a computer screen used to make images and words. With today's amazing display technologies, such as the "retina display" for the new iPad and MacBook Pro, these pixels are so small they make the experience of reading sheet music on a computer screen incredibly vibrant and – many might argue – better than reading on physical paper. Of course, there's no arguing how much easier it is to read a digital screen in low light than a piece of paper music under an anemic, underpowered stand light!

Cutting-edge display technologies aside, here are 10 additional reasons why using computers to read music is better than paper:

1. Eliminate bulk

A single 1.2-pound, 16-gig iPad (the smallest and cheapest model available) can hold the equivalent of *60,000 pages* of paper. That's comes out to 600 pounds of physical paper! Next time you lug around your heavy binders and gig books, I promise that your aching muscles will remember that fact (I'll give you the names of my massage therapist and chiropractor).

2. Never lose music

Classical composers wrote works that ranged in length from 1-2 page miniatures to massive symphonies filling hundreds of pages. If we average each work of a classical composer to be 20 pages each, a single 16-gigabyte iPad would contain all the compositions of Vivaldi, J.S. Bach, Mozart, Beethoven and Chopin, with room to spare. Imagine, all that genius in an approximately 9.5x7.5x.37-inch tablet! With that kind of storage, it becomes easy to simply carry your entire music library with you wherever you go, and never worry about misplacing your music or remembering to bring a part.

3. Find music instantly

I used to have these huge wall units to house my paper sheet-music collection, with all the works catalogued in boxes alphabetized by composer. Even then, it would take a considerable investment in time and effort to find all the pieces I needed for the day's rehearsals, lessons and performances. By the end of the school year, I'd have to search through a ridiculous mountain of music stacked on top of my piano.

A friend of mine watched a phenomenal jazz set come to a screeching halt as the drummer scrambled for five minutes through a stack of sheet music the size of a New York City phone book looking for the next number. With digital music, you just type a few keystrokes and, *voilà*, instantly there's any piece in your collection you need. We'll talk more later about ways to organize your digital collection. You can pull up all your works by the name of a song, the composer name, or even the key signature, tempo, genre/style, and other descriptions practically before everyone else is done wetting their finger.

4. Make automatic set lists

Ever have your set list (that list of the songs or pieces to be performed in order at a gig or concert) blow away in a strong breeze? Or spill your drink on it, making it read like recently unearthed hieroglyphics? That's so yesterday. Now, rather than having to shuffle books or physically re-order pages in a binder, you can easily search and select your set list songs on your digital device, change their order on the fly, and have the songs appear automatically in order during the show as if they were part of a single book. All you need is a digital music-reading app. We'll go into more detail about setting up set lists with various apps in chapter 24.

5. Transpose music instantly

One of my biggest fears as an accompanist was to have the singer I was working with come down with a cold and ask to transpose down a couple of keys right on the spot. With certain types of music (text-based lyrics and chord charts) and reading apps designed around dynamic music notation (Sibelius, Finale, etc.), changing keys on the fly is as simple as a few taps on the screen. You'll come off a genius. Chapter 30 will cover apps for reading text-based sheet-music; chapter 27 will cover proprietary sheet-music reader apps, many with the ability to transpose music purchased from online publishers; and chapter 33 will go over music notation software and their accompanying reader apps.

6. Mark up your music with rainbow colors

Brain scientists point out that the use of bright, contrasting colors contributes to faster learning and better memory retention. Digital music makes it easy to add brightly colored "ink" and transparent highlights to your music. And it can be easily erased. Ready to throw out your collection of color sharpies, White-Out, and lead pencils with worn-out erasers? Jump to the start of the digital rainbow in chapter 20.

7. Eliminate blind spots

If you are reading music that requires at least one page turn, you have a "blind spot" – you can't see what comes next until you turn the page. With certain apps, you can set up the page turns so that the screen shows the bottom half of the previous page and the top half of the next page, creating a continuous "look-ahead" view. How much better would that be for learning music, and keeping a smooth sense of flow and phrasing? For a sneak peak ahead, go to chapter 21.

8. Enlarge your music

Have the wrinkles around your eyes become as deep as desert arroyos from squinting at your sheet music under a low-wattage light? When your music is in a digital format, your view of the music is only limited by the size of your screen and the application used to display it. Some programs even give you the option to see zoomed views of your music half a page at a time (this works particularly well for screens that are horizontal, such as laptops or desktop monitors). Other apps can work with music that has been digitally cropped to show even larger views of your music – as little as one or two measures at a time. Text-based music readers give you the option to change font size and properties. Sound like a godsend, Mr. Magoo? Start your musical growth spurt in chapter 19, and then for more giant goodness, look at appendices A, B, and C.

9. Turn everyone else's pages

With the iPad, there are several apps that enable a master iPad to control any number of slave iPads, so that the master can open the same song on every slave, and in some cases even turn pages for everyone. Talk about keeping everyone on the same page! Talk about power! Just think of how you could mess with their heads! For the super-secret skinny on megalomaniacal musical control, jump to the evil laugh in chapter 24.

10. Turn pages hands free

Ever wish you had a third hand? If you use both hands to play an instrument, you have – for all intents and purposes – a disability when it comes to turning pages. With digital sheet music, not only do you have a wide variety of software options for viewing and working with your music, but you can get hardware for turning your pages hands free, either with wireless digital page-turning pedals, or even other controllers such as bite and tongue switches – rather like eating the score! Now you can keep your hands on your instrument and your focus on the music. And, yes, we'll get into more detail about setting up hands-free page-turning options in chapter 35.

CHAPTER THREE

A Short History Of Digital Sheet-Music Readers

Finale 3.0 Box Cover, circa 1995

Generally speaking, in the past reading sheet music on computer monitors and laptop screens was like trying to fit size-12 feet into size-7 shoes: a bad fit, painfully uncomfortable, and probably the source for mental or emotional bunions.

I remember a box cover for an early version of the venerable music-notation software, Finale, on which a blissful pianist is basking in the glow of reading his digital score on a ginormous cathode-tube computer monitor that's perched like a cyborg hippo atop his grand piano. Back then, screens were expensive, small, and oriented in an "unmusical" way, displaying pages horizontally ("landscape" in computer-speak) rather than the way that most sheet music is printed, vertically ("portrait"). Reading sheet music on a typical computer screen meant either zooming out to an impractical level to fit a vertical page on a horizontal screen, or reading small segments of a page at a time, which was a problem if your music staff happened to fall right in the middle of the break point, cutting off notes below or above.

The Toshiba Portégé M200, one of the first convertible Tablet PCs

Tablet PCs, introduced by Microsoft back in 2001, were the first computers to begin to solve this reading-orientation problem. The early ones came in two designs: a laptop design, in which the screen could be flipped around and folded backwards over the keyboard; or the "slate" design that had no external keyboard at all (there was an on-screen virtual keyboard). The latter made you input information by drawing or tapping on the screen with a digital pen. Both designs gave users the option to rotate the view in both horizontal and vertical positions. Reading a full page of digital music right-side up became practical for the first time. I was approaching digital nirvana!

These tablet PCs were terrific for geeks like me, but they were prohibitively expensive and never really caught on with the general public. The price alone probably killed the possibility of mass adoption, but I'm sure that the Windows operating system didn't help (painful for me to admit, as I've been a longtime Windows fan).

Despite the tablet PC's great digital-pen inking and handwriting-recognition features, Windows was really intended for keyboard and mouse input, not direct input by human hands. Ok, watching a handwritten sentence get recognized as text was pretty cool, I admit, but impractically slow. Pecking out a sentence with a digital pen on the tablet PC's onscreen keyboard was laughable, like one-finger typing with that finger in a splint. Other eggs to throw: their bulky size, lousy battery life, and screens dimmed by scratch-resistant coatings to prevent them from looking like overused Etch-A-Sketch toys. One *could* read music on these things, but it wasn't very pleasant. Nonetheless, someone out there knew that we geeks were willing to endure hefty credit-card debt and put up with such shortcomings just because the technology hinted at tantalizingly possibilities. Something in our genes, I suppose.

Next evolutionary jump

In December, 2001, *ta-da,* Freehand Systems produced a digital-music reader it called the MusicPad Pro that was years ahead of its time in concept, but woefully hobbled by the technologies of its time. It featured a 12.1-inch pressure touchscreen, giving users the ability to annotate scores and turn pages with the tap of a finger or with a wired pedal. The MusicPad Pro was eerily prescient of the Amazon Kindle and Apple iPad with regard to – allow me to lapse into a little geek-speak here – its ambitious attempt at creating a complete ecosystem between a hardware reading device and a proprietary digital sheet-music store, to which it directly connected.

Freehand System's MusicPad Pro

But, alas, once again, price was a serious killjoy. Users paid $1,000 for what basically amounted to a one-trick pony in a kludgy form with lousy battery life. But, boy, did Freehand try mightily to market it. The company got endorsements from famous bands like "Yes," and classical musicians like violinist Itzhak Perlman (who I'm sure never used the device more than once). It even hosted a media event by the Chicago Symphony using the MusicPad Pro in performance. Sadly, the device never evolved beyond its first version design and died a William Shatner-esque death (you know, slow, very drawn-out). Its final spasm was the MusicPad Maestro, intended for conductors with a larger screen and a conductor's ego-sized price point.

The first Amazon Kindle

In 2007, things began to get rolling in earnest: Amazon introduced the Kindle. With its small-form factor, battery life measured in weeks instead of hours, seamless ability to wirelessly purchase and download electronic books, and its ground-breaking use of E-Ink technology (this made reading the screen more like reading actual paper), the Kindle began to put digital reading on our mental maps. But – a pox upon their house – for musicians the screen was much too small, and the page "turns" had a strange delay, making it an impractical device for reading music, particularly in real-time performance. Picture it – here you are in the throes of a high-speed Tarantella or Metallica thrash. You read the notes, press the page-turn button, wait and wait for the blinking screen refresh ... aaarrgghh ... another train wreck! And since the Kindle was intended primarily as a read-only device, there was really no pragmatic way to annotate pages. Another one-trick pony. But this time Amazon got it right for its intended market of book readers, and it had a much friendlier price point and feature set.

Then ... cue the 1812 Overture Finale ... there was Apple!

The Apple iPad

In 2010, Apple introduced the iPad (which actually was conceptualized before the iPhone, if you are a trivia buff). The iPad learned the lessons from its predecessors, stepped up to the plate and knocked one out of the park – the first iPad sold 300,000 units on its first day of sale; the iPad 2, a year later, sold 500,000 its first day; and in 2012, the new iPad with its deservedly hyped "retina display" sold a staggering 1,000,000 units on its first sale day. As of this writing, iPads are on track to be in the hands of over 102 million users in the USA alone. Almost 1 in 3 Americans owns one. It's not hard to figure out why the incredible ecosystem of "apps" (a shortened version of the word "applications," coined by Apple – Apple/App, get it? – and hardware peripherals for iPads exploded almost overnight.

Very likely, you either already own an iPad or know someone who does, so in some ways I may be preaching to the choir. But since I am intending to help musicians find digital solutions for reading sheet music, I'd like to point out why the iPad works particularly well as a musician's reading tool. Let's stand the digital contestants next to each other and ask them to show off their stuff (We'll forgo the swimsuit portion):

1. Vavavoom (the form factor)

Where the tablet PC and MusicPad Pro were relatively bulky and heavy, the iPad is thin and light, weighing in at approximatcly 1.2 pounds (this varies depending on the model. The first iPad was the heaviest. The new iPad mini looks like an adorable digital Chihuahua next to its older kin). The iPad also boasts a battery life of 10 hours, which far outperforms the older machines' output of 2-3 hours. That means you can leave the power cord at home during long days of rehearsals or gigs – less bulk in your gig bag.

While larger than a typical Kindle (leaving the iPad mini out of the picture temporarily), the iPad's 9-inch screen is noticeably smaller than the tablet PC or MusicPad Pro, both of which sported 12.1-inch screens that more closely resembled the size of a typical 8.5x11″ sheet of music paper (if you're musician with poor vision ... aside, "Magoo" ... we'll address your cool app solutions and hardware alternatives later). On the other hand, the screen quality of the iPad is bright, clear, and vibrant (superfabulously with the new iPad) – so much so, that some folks argue that reading music on an iPad is much easier on the eyes than physical paper (envision playing in a dark night club, or being jammed into an orchestra pit with finicky music-stand lights. Now picture an evenly backlit iPad ... you can stop squinting now).

2. From Clunk to Class

The tablet PC required a digital pen to operate the screen. Using my tablet PCs in my early paperless days, my biggest fear was misplacing or losing that pesky pen, leaving me dead in the water right before an important performance with no way to navigate or open my sheet-music files. My solution was to lash my pens to my tablet PCs with dental floss. That way, at least, I could always be ready to perform with a smile (no groaning, please). The other major problem with the tablet PC was the painful 5-minute boot-up process before one could actually *do* anything. Well, it did give me an opportunity to floss.

The MusicPad Pro came with a touchscreen that could be used with either a plastic stylus or a firm finger press, which was a slightly better solution than a pen-only computer. Still, you needed to keep a close eye (or a piece of dental floss) on that stylus. Using your finger was about as effective as trying to scratch an itch through a leather jacket. And you had to be careful not to let your wrist touch the screen while using the stylus, since it could only accept one pressure point at a time.

But, with the iPad's cool touchscreen technology you could even use multiple fingers at the same time. And unlike the MusicPad Pro's pressure-based input screen technology, the iPad had a zippy response to the lightest of touches. Begone pens and dental floss! Quite a "magical" feeling, as Steve Jobs and his cohorts loved to say. And turning on the iPad does NOT require a trip to the water cooler while waiting for the machine to boot up. Press the home or power button on the iPad and it's ON instantly. Amazing how such a simple concept could be so revolutionary!

3. Show Us Your Stuff (or who knew I needed that?)

In 2003, Apple introduced the iTunes store, an online resource for buying music as MP3 files, a format that compresses music to about 10 times smaller than digital music files used to be, so that you don't have to go take a nap while the music is downloading. With the iTunes Store came a seamless way to easily, affordably and, most importantly, legally purchase music and instantly download it to computers and Apple's iPod. This laid the foundation for the App Store, opened as an iTunes update on July 10, 2008. Now users could not only get content – aka, music, audio books, movies, and the like – but also a whole world of programs to do nifty things with iPhones, iPods, and of course, the titular iPad.

You have to admit, this was a stroke of genius. The big argument, PC stuff vs. Apple stuff, always before went something like this:

Apple guy: "Look how cool this is, and how easy it is to use!"

PC guy: "Harummph. But Apple is so arrogant that it won't share its source codes (the little elves inside that make everything run), so you can't get other stuff that works on my PC to work with your computer. Nyaah, nyaah."

Ah, but Apple's products were so well designed, and were becoming so popular that programmers' eyes began flashing dollar signs (instead of their usual 1s and 0s). They began making serious money by creating apps, and hardware manufacturers began making i-accessories. All of a sudden, these digital denizens saw the monolithic Apple designs and the company's alleged arrogance as a great thing. Uniformity in design means you don't have to design dozens of variations of the same product. The result? Incredible diversity of options for the user of Apple products. Ironically, now i-users have access to the widest variety of ways to work with their devices, far more than other tablets and mobile reading devices on the market.

Did someone say "Nyaah, nyaah?"

4. How Much Did You Say You Cost?

So, back in 2001, the one-trick pony MusicPad Pro cost a whopping $1,000 – chump change for Janet Jackson or the Backstreet Boys, but way beyond the typical mortal musician's budget. Many models of tablet PCs started out around $1,500, a price point to make even Warren Buffet squirm (well, maybe not, since he and Bill Gates are chums). The iPad, on the other hand, begins at $499 for the 16-gig model (and $329 for the diminutive iPad mini), a much more appealing price point. Some musicians argue this is still too expensive, but isn't it really a matter of perspective and priorities? You don't hesitate to plunk down thousands of dollars for an instrument or hundreds of dollars for an amp or some other tool to enhance your sound. Shouldn't your reading tools be framed similarly? A digital music reader will reap enormous benefits in the long run towards enhancing your musicianship. We'll look at that "return on your investment" in later chapters.

The iPad isn't perfect for all musicians as a digital reader, but for many it is a great starting point. It does many things very nicely in a form factor that's easy to use. Because of this, we'll spend a good bit of time in this book using the iPad as a launching point for digital sheet-music reading. But as nice as the iPad is, I would be remiss if I didn't take a moment to point out the massive horde of alternative tablets quickly bearing down on the hapless musician, offering a bewildering array of hardware, software, and – in some cases – wallet-friendlier options.

Rise of the Androids and Return of the Pen

Android and Microsoft follow Apple's Lead

As is inevitable with any wildly popular product, the market soon saw a deluge of manufacturers jumping at the new opportunities carved out by the runaway success of the iPad. In 2007, search-engine giant Google introduced a new operating system for smartphones called Android. What made Android markedly different from Apple's operating system for iPads and iPhones was its open nature – rather than trying to exert draconian control over every aspect of software and hardware a la Steve Jobs and enforce a strict uniformity between devices and user experiences, Android was designed to be an open system, meaning that manufacturers and developers could take what they liked and tweak the operating system to their hearts' content.

The result was an explosion of styles, sizes, shapes, and even flavors (Google likes to nickname each new version of Android after a dessert – Cupcake, Donut, Eclair, and most recently Honeycomb, Ice Cream Sandwich, and two flavors of Jelly Bean – I'm personally waiting for the "Chocolate Covered Espresso Bean" flavor). Following Apple's lead, Google introduced Android for tablets in 2011, leaving it up to a motley mix of manufacturers to come up with their own hardware to run the cavity-inducing operating system flavors. The first Android tablets, to be blunt, were pretty lousy, and I'm sure the Cupertino crew could be heard chortling snide comparisons and laughing fruit juice through their nostrils. But jump forward to 2012, and suddenly those Apple guys aren't laughing anymore, as sales of Android tablets began to overtake iPads.

Meanwhile, the Microsoft empire was preparing to strike back with tablets of their own. In late 2012, Microsoft introduced the Surface, a re-envisioned tablet with a cool magnetic clickity snap-on keyboard cover and a radically redesigned operating system, Windows RT. Surface attempted to provide a hybrid user experience between touch and desktop interfaces, in a hardware design that tried to follow Apple's paradigm of being developed and manufactured completely in-house, as opposed to relying on other hardware manufactures as Microsoft had done in the past. But to make a short story even shorter, Windows RT was a bust – sales of the tablet with the stunted operating system akin to an awkward tween with braces and a bad case of acne flopped, since it couldn't run full Windows programs and didn't really have any significant apps of its own.

Ah, but Microsoft's second salvo in the beginning of 2013 came roaring into the market with the introduction of the full version of Windows 8 running on the Surface Pro. With the Surface Pro came a return to Microsoft's tablet PC's roots, in a sense: the inclusion of an awesome digital pen, in addition to touchscreen capabilities and the ability to run full versions of Windows programs, not just apps custom-coded for an anemic operating system. While still far behind in the tablet race, the Surface Pro has managed to capture 4% of the market in breakneck speed as of this writing. And with Microsoft being Microsoft, the Windows 8 operating system can be found running on tablets and tablet convertibles made from a growing number of manufacturers like Samsung and Lenovo and others.

Tablet pens, by the way, can also be found with Android tablets made by Samsung in their stylish Galaxy Note series. This might help to account why Samsung is now nipping hotly at Apple's heels as the number-two manufacturer of tablets.

So what does this headache-inducing tablet market analysis have to do with musicians considering digital sheet-music options? Simply, that the world is now a Petri dish of more hardware and software options than ever before, and that you should be patting yourself on the back for holding this book in your hands to help guide you to the digital sheet-music-reader solution that will best fit your needs.

Onward!

CHAPTER FOUR

What Do I Need to Get Started Reading Sheet Music Digitally?

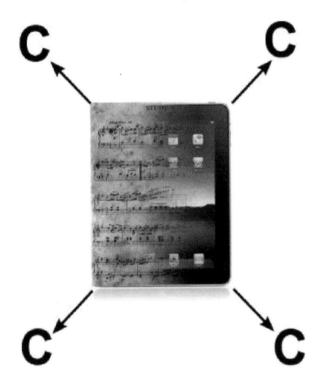

All right, enough with the back story, let's get down to business. You are nervous, a little daunted, but nonetheless convinced that it's time to go digital. Been there, done that, so I think I know what questions you're probably asking right now.

    – Which computer is right for me?

    – How do I get music into my computer?

    – What programs do I need?

    – Besides a computer, what other equipment will I need?

    – Given the rate at which technology changes, how can I be sure that the equipment I invest in won't be obsolete within a few years?

Let's address the last question first. As of this writing, I will have been a "paperless pianist" for nearly 12 years. Even though the computers and equipment that I've used to store, read and annotate my digital sheet-music scores have changed many times over during that time period, it's amazing to me that the very first digital-music files I scanned from my paper sources still look perfectly pristine, while the physical paper versions have already started to yellow and crumble. In other words, stop worrying.

We know that computer technology changes on almost a daily basis (for a quick reminder, re-read my headache-inducing analysis of the tablet market explosion at the end of chapter 3). The good news is this isn't as important as you might think. If you know how to take care of a musical instrument (you know, not driving away with it on the roof of your car, changing out the valve pads on your horn, etc), you can apply that same level of understanding to maintaining your digital sheet-music-reading-computer for many years to come. And you'll be better educated on the best computers to upgrade to when necessary.

And get this: You've heard of Internet cloud storage services like Dropbox and iCloud, haven't you? These are places out there in the wild blue (actually in cyberspace) that will store a copy of everything on your computer, so you really don't even have to worry about being completely dependent on a single computer device anymore.

Here's an easy way to remember the things you need to know – "four Cs," the four categories you'll need to get started.

1. Computer
2. Content
3. Containers
4. Controllers

Easy, yes (like laying a piano in C major)? So here we go.

1. Computer (picking your plastic)

Ask yourself these questions:

– How much mobility do I need?

– How big does the screen need to be in order for me to see it?

– What is the meaning of life (just kidding ... wanted to see if you were still awake)?

– How many accessories am I going to need to support my computer (containers, controllers and the like)? Of course, it's too soon for you to really know that, but patience, dear person, we'll get there.

While tablet computers such as the iPad might be great for many musicians due to their portability and ease of use, other musicians who don't need to be mobile (like organists or teachers working in studios) might be better off with laptops, desktop computers connected to larger monitors, or even large touchscreen computers. We'll drill down this topic starting in chapter 16, "How to Select the Perfect Computer for Reading Digital Sheet Music." Meanwhile, just think about it.

2. Content (other than your favorite comic books)

By content, I mean both the type of music you work with and the sources where your music can be found. For instance, classical musicians work with content based on traditional music notation containing staff lines, key signatures, notes and rests. Musicians in more popular genres work with content based mainly on text, such as lyrics, chord symbols and tablatures. Your preferred content will determine both where you find your music sources and how you get that content into your digital sheet-music computer, ranging from scans of physical books and binders to direct downloads from online sheet-music resources.

This will also determine which programs are best suited for your content needs, and what kind of interactivity you will need from your music – will you be using PDF files to draw annotations on your music? (If you don't know, these are files that are more like photos. You can't really go into them and change type, but you can mark them up.) Or will you use a text reader so that you can change your font sizes and transpose chord symbols on the fly? Or will you use a proprietary reader for computerized music notation from programs like Finale or Sibelius? Don't panic ... we'll talk more about this starting in chapter 22.

3. Containers (How do I position this thing so it doesn't crash to the floor in the middle of the quiet section of the music?)

By containers, I mean hardware accessories used to hold or mount your computer, turning it for all intents and purposes into a digital music stand. This may or may not be relevant to a classical pianist, who can usually count on a music rack built in to his instruments to hold his tablet or support his laptop. But guitarists or orchestral musicians will almost always need a way to safely mount their computers, especially if the oboist who sits in front of you weighs 300 lbs. Container options vary widely depending on the type of computer being used. We'll explore some of the current options in chapter 34.

4. Controllers (as in, "Hey fellers, watch this!")

Controllers are hardware accessories that enable you to work with your digital sheet music in a variety of ways, ranging from digital pens for drawing annotations, to pedals and other switches that let you turn pages without using your hands. Some computer devices, like the iPad, don't require digital pens to draw on the screen, whereas some tablets and tablet PCs already come bundled with such pens. Page-turning pedals and switches, on the other hand, are a relatively new accessory that most musicians don't think of until they're confronted with the stark experience of viewing their music one digital page at a time and have to consider how to get to the next digital "page" in ways that don't necessitate finger swiping, mouse clicking, or puzzled head-scratching. Our tour of the wonderful world of digital sheet music controllers meets up in chapter 35. As a special preview, we'll look at some examples soon of various types of musicians and the 4-C configurations that best fit their needs starting in chapter 10.

CHAPTER FIVE

The 5th C: The Art of Converting Paper to PDFs

We've looked at four general categories of tools that a musician will need to read music digitally, what I call the "4 C's": Computer, Content, Container, and Controller. When it comes to the second C – Content – the type of music you work with will greatly determine the means with which you will get your music into your digital-reading computer of choice. There is a wealth of sheet-music content available on the Internet for instant download – no need to wait for the mailman to deliver to your house or favorite music store. For many musicians, this will be the first place to look, and oftentimes there's no need to bother with paper versions. We'll touch on a number of popular online resources for digital sheet music in a variety of genres in a later chapter.

But perhaps you are a musician using paper sheet music that can't be found in any digital format anywhere on the Internet. Maybe you are working with paper versions that are marked up with precious fingerings and special instructions that are more valuable than the music itself. In that case, you will need to learn the art of a "5th C": **Conversion**. By conversion, I mean hardware and software tools used to convert your paper music into digital files that can then be read and worked on in your reading app or program of choice.

There are basically three steps in the conversion process:

1. Scan
2. Process
3. Transfer

Let's take a closer look at each of these steps.

Scan

To scan is to convert a physical document into a digital format. Basically, you are creating a digital photo of the document, using a hardware device called a Scanner. Scanners come in all shapes and sizes, and are sometimes part of an "all-in-one" office machine that can print, fax, make copies, and make a perfect double soy latte (I'm kidding about that last feature). The type of physical music you need to convert will determine the kind of scanner you will want to work with. Here are three general types of scanners and the types of music they are best suited for:

1. Flatbed – these are scanners that have a glass surface on which to place your music, and a lid to prevent you from being blinded by the scanner's light. Flatbeds are best suited for music books and bound collections, and usually require a connection to a laptop or desktop computer to process and transfer the digitized images.

Brother MFC-400CN scanner printer

2. Sheet-fed – these are scanners that are much more compact and tend to look like plastic rolling pins. Sheet-fed scanners are best suited for single sheets of music, since only one page can be fed into the scanner at a time. These types of scanners also require a connection to a laptop or desktop computer, although as of this writing, there is a new sheet-fed scanner called the iConvert Scanner that has a slot for your iPad to sit in and receive the scans directly. http://www.brookstone.com/iconvert-ipad-scanner

iConvert Scanner for iPad from Brookstone

3. App – Believe it or not, smartphone cameras are becoming good enough to create sharp, legible scans of music. You'll need the latest smartphones with high-resolution cameras (the latest iPhones from Apple work beautifully, as well as the latest offerings from the various Android smartphone manufacturers) and apps like TurboScan for the iPhone or CamScanner for the Android phones. (Note: while the iPad 2 and the "new" iPads [3 & 4] also have cameras, the resolution isn't as high on either of these devices as the ones you'll find on the latest smartphone cameras. The new iPad's camera is a lot better than the iPad 2's, but there's no flash for low light situations, and you might find it hard to hold your iPad steady without a dedicated mount. More on that later). Scanning apps are best for smaller songs or scanning on the fly when you need to digitize your music in a pinch and don't have access to the other kinds of hardware scanners. Keep in mind that if you're trying to scan pages from a bound book that you'll have to deal with the curvature of the binding, especially if the book is brand new.

Scanning with a smartphone

Process

Every scanner and scanning app will have different settings and options, so you'll have to refer to their instructions for the specifics on processing your scanned page images. We're going to want to aim for the following goals:

1. Create a universal file that can be read on as many computers and programs or apps as possible
2. If you are scanning more than one page for a song, then this file will need to be able to have multiple "pages"
3. Make the file as legible as possible
4. Make sure the file is as small as possible to ensure that it loads on any computer quickly and that the page turns (if necessary) are fast
5. Make sure that the file name is descriptive enough for easy cataloging and searches

Thanks to a company called Adobe, the most universal file format since 1993 has been the Portable Document Format, or PDF for short. PDF files were designed to be read universally on every computer, which is why I've been able to keep up with the rapid changes in computer technologies since my conversion to a paperless lifestyle in 2001.

All my scanned music consists of PDF files, and as I mentioned before, the remarkable thing is that the very first music files I scanned are still as pristine looking as the day I created them, as opposed to their physical counterparts, which have sadly yellowed and in many cases already started to crumble. PDF files have the ability to contain multiple pages – some of my music, after all, is 50-100+ pages in length.

Most scanners these days have the option to directly create multi-page PDF files. If not, don't despair; here are some software options for converting image files created from your scanner into multi-page PDF files:

iCombiner for Mac

This is a great program that does just what its name describes, and it's free to boot! You can take any kind of image or document file, drag them into iCombiner's program box, rearrange the pages in any order you like, press a button, and spit out a single multi-page PDF file.

http://download.cnet.com/iCombiner/
3000-2094_4-190014.html

PrimoPDF for Windows

PrimoPDF is a free program that will give you the ability to virtually "print" image and document files into a single multi-page PDF. Unlike iCombiner, you can't mix and match different types of files (images with Word document files, for example), but as long as you work with a single file type you can convert almost anything into a multi-page PDF.

http://download.cnet.com/PrimoPDF/
3000-18497_4-10264577.html?tag=mncol;1

To make your scanned pages legible and as small in file size as possible, you will want to look for options on your scanner to scan in black and white. Scanning in color will make your file look great, but you'll have to deal with a much larger file size, which can choke the loading and page-turning speeds, especially if you're using a computer with a slow processor (like the original iPad 1). Grayscale, while smaller than color formats, still creates a file size that's unwieldy, especially if your song is more than two or three pages in length.

You will also want to set the scan DPI to either 150 or 300. DPI stands for "dots per inch," and represents the resolution or how fine the image quality of the scan will be. Photographers and printers want a high DPI, but for music-reading purposes the extra dots are unnecessary. In fact, if you find that your staff lines are getting broken up with your scans, you may want to try a DPI as low as 75 – the scanning software will tend to consolidate fine lines better at lower resolutions. Since every scanner and scanning app is different, you'll want to experiment with a few different DPI settings to find what is optimal for your reading purposes and computer performance. Keep in mind that the higher the DPI, the larger the file size, so you'll want to find the right balance between legibility and performance (loading and page-turning speed) for your needs. Most of my music is scanned at 300 DPI, so feel free to use that as a benchmark.

Finally, you'll want to come up with a naming convention for your files that best suits your particular musical needs. As a classical collaborative pianist, my primary title needs are as follows:

1. **Composer name** (usually just the last name will suffice, or in special cases – like with the Bach family – the last name and the initial of the first name. And perhaps the middle name as well, right, J.C.? Or was it J.S.?).
2. **Title of the piece.** If there is no title, then I'll indicate what type of piece it is (Sonata, Concerto, etc.) followed by a number (if there are multiple versions of the same type of piece) and

key signature. (See #4 below for an exception to this order).

3. **Publisher's catalogue info** – these include general indications like Opus and Number (Op and No for short), or unique catalogue references in the cases of particular composers, such as J. S. Bach (BWV number) or Mozart (K number).

4. Since I work with such a wide variety of instrumentalists, I need to include the **primary instrument** for which the piece was written. If the piece is for my own instrument (piano), I won't bother, but if it's for another instrument, in many cases, I'll actually put the instrument name before the title.

Here are a few examples of some of the PDF file names I use in my library:

Chopin Ballade No 1 in G minor, Op 23
Bach, JS Violin Concerto in E major, BWV 1042
Massenet Meditation from Thais for Violin and Piano

Did you notice something in the above titles? I tried to avoid using periods and special non-alphanumeric symbols, such as a period after "No" or "Op". In computer language, periods are generally used to separate between the name title of a file and the extension that indicates what sort of file it is. For example, the full file name of the Chopin Ballade is actually:

Chopin Ballade No 1 in G minor Op 23.pdf

Note the ".pdf" at the end – that tells the computer that it is looking at a PDF file, and will assign the appropriate compatible program to open it.

I also try to avoid symbols like ; : # " ? ! ( ) & + This came as a result of working with some pretty old Windows programs that didn't have the ability to include those symbols as naming conventions. Since I want to be able to read my files as universally as possible, just to be safe I generally try to stick with using only alphanumeric characters.

As you can gather, classical music is quite complicated, hence the convoluted naming convention. For folks who play more popular genres like jazz, rock, pop, or worship songs, you may not need anything more than the title of the song or, perhaps in some cases, the name of the band or artist that made the song famous as well. Determine what works best for you, and think about the information you would need to be able to call up the song on your computer quickly and easily.

Seem like a lot to absorb? Never fear, in practice, it's actually not very difficult at all. Once you have your equipment and settings established and know how you want to name your files, you'll find yourself to be a Master of Conversion in no time.

The Lazy Musician's Option: Book-Scanning Services

If the thought of scanning hundreds or thousands of pages of music books is about as appealing to you as organizing receipts for an IRS audit, then you might want to consider book-scanning services like 1DollarScan.com. No, I don't work for these guys, but I like their idea of making book scanning as cheap and easy as possible! Keep in mind, there are two types of book-scanning services: destructive, and non-destructive. Destructive services cut the binding of your book and recycle what's left over after scanning. You don't get the book back, but it's about half the cost of non-destructive scanning. If your books are too precious, then consider non-destructive scanning services.

On the other hand, if you are giddy with the thought of reclaiming precious wall space within your overpriced New York City bungalow, then consider destructive scanning services like 1DollarScan.com. Be sure to overwhelm whatever book-scanning service you hire with your newfangled knowledge of image format, DPI, and naming conventions for your PDF files, then have your private butler Jeeves fetch the wheelbarrow, cart off your music book collection to the post office, and drum your fingers petulantly as you wait for the PDF files to be delivered to you by email or CD.

The Over-Achieving Musician's Option: DIY Book Scanning

If you're the kind of musician that gets their kicks out of a Schenkerian analysis of Morton Feldman's 6+ hour-long String Quartet II, or memorizing the entire oeuvre of Scarlatti 555 sonatas, then you might have some fun and giggles making your own high-speed/high-volume book scanner, similar to the devices used by the likes of Google and Amazon.

A homemade book scanner from www.diybookscanner.org

If you have the patience, building chops, and gee-whiz geeky curiosity, you can find free instructions for building one of these contraptions at www.diybookscanner.org. The site's organizers claim that you can scan a staggering 1,200 pages an hour with such a system, and that you won't have to cut up or mangle your books in the process. The basic components are as follows:

1. Lighting
2. Two digital cameras (one can be used, but two is ideal for working twice as fast)
3. Camera support
4. Platen (a V-shaped "page flattener" made out of glass or acrylic)

5. Cradle for holding the book

6. Base for holding everything together

7. Electronics for triggering the cameras

You can even find links for free software at the above site to process the photographed images in a jiffy and port them into your preferred reading file format.

Of course, if you have $50,000 taking up too much space in your wallet, you could always invest in a commercial version like the Kirtas KABIS family of robotic book scanners.

The Kirtas KABIS IIIW Robotic Book Scanner

Then again, maybe $300 in raw materials and a bit of elbow grease isn't such a bad idea after all...

In our next chapters, we're going to take an in-depth look at various ways to transfer your scanned files into your reading computer and app or program of choice. In a preview nutshell, you will generally have the following transfer options:

1. Via Internet (email, Dropbox, etc.)

2. Via physical connection (USB docking cable + iTunes for the iPad, or a memory card/stick from computer to computer)

Onwards, intrepid musician!

CHAPTER SIX

Transferring Converted Music to an iPad Using Email

Once you have your sheet music converted into a digital PDF file using a scanner or scanning app, or your butler Jeeves carting off your collection to a book-scanning service (see the previous chapter on converting paper sheet music to PDF files), we need to find a way to get that file from the computer used to scan the music to the device that you will use to read and work with that file.

If you are using the same desktop or laptop computer that you scanned the music with, then you can skip this chapter (we'll talk about various programs for Mac and PC computers to read your sheet music PDF files). If you want to move that file to your iPad, then stick around – we're going to look at a number of ways to do this. (For Android tablet users, jump to chapter 9).

One way to transfer a digital sheet-music file into your iPad is via email, particularly if you are using a scanning app on a smartphone. You will want to make sure that you have your email settings established in your iPad's default email app (this is usually done as soon as you turn on your iPad for the very first time. If you skipped this part for some reason, tap on the "Settings" app icon, then on the left hand column, tap on "Mail, Contacts, Calendars" and follow the instructions under the "Accounts" menu box).

Email the sheet-music PDF file to yourself as an attachment. On your iPad, tap the mail app icon, then look for the email message you just sent yourself. You should see your email message with your PDF file attachment as follows:

Tap on the icon that represents the PDF attachment to open it in the mail app's browser. It will appear as follows:

On the upper right hand corner, tap on the icon that looks like an arrow coming out of a box. This will bring up the option to select which app you want to open the PDF file with. Doing so will bring up a "default" PDF reading app (if you have one installed). It will look like this:

If you want to open the PDF file in a different app, tap on "Open In...." You will then be given a selection of PDF-compatible apps to select. You can use your finger to scroll down or up the provided list. Scroll down until you find your preferred PDF reading app. In this instance, I'm scrolling down to select a popular app called forScore:

Once your desired app is selected, you will see it appear in that app. In the following image, you can see that the PDF file has been automatically added to the forScore library:

This email method works best for transferring digital sheet music files one at a time. In the next chapter, we'll look at another way to wirelessly transfer scanned PDF sheet-music files to your iPad in larger batches.

By the way, you may want to take a look at the following interactive App Guide for some recommendations on various apps for your music-reading needs (http://airturn.com/appguide):

CHAPTER SEVEN

Transferring Converted Music to an iPad Using Dropbox

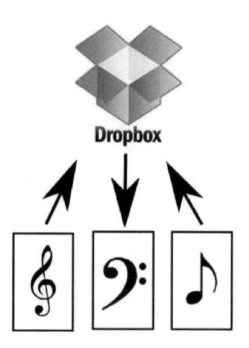

When I first started using computers to store and read all my music, my biggest fear was tripping on stage, smashing my computer, and losing my entire digital library in one fell swoop. This actually happened to me once right in the middle of a major concert! I left my slate Tablet PC on the piano during intermission. One of the stage hands closed the music rack without realizing my computer was still perched on it, and it flew off with a thunderous crash and a deafening collective gasp from the audience.

Miraculously, the computer – screen and all – remained perfectly intact, but that was enough to give me a mild heart attack! I used USB thumb drives and portable hard drives of all shapes and sizes to carry and back up my library, but being the absent-minded musician that I am, I found myself constantly misplacing and losing them.

One of the most amazing bits of technology in recent years has been the development of the "cloud". Thanks to greater availability and increasing speeds of Internet connectivity, you no longer need to depend on the fickle nature of your own physical hard drives or worry about your own butterfingers to keep a steady grip on your precious data. Online web-based storage solutions have been around for a good while, but one particular service – Dropbox (www.dropbox.com) – revolutionized the ease and convenience of keeping your files in the cloud. Founded in 2007 and officially launched in 2008, Dropbox can be installed on virtually any computer device and automatically synchronizes your files between your machines. Best of all, Dropbox is free for the first 5 Gigs of storage space – throw away those thumb drives! Of course, you can pay for more space if you really like the service, but you can also grow your storage capacity if you refer others to join (500 MB per friend, Baby!)

Dropbox is a popular feature with several iPad apps, giving you the ability to store, download, share and sync your sheet-music files right from inside the app. Each app handles Dropbox connectivity differently, so you'll have to take some time to explore each app's idiosyncrasies. Nevertheless, this is a great way to transfer and manage relatively large digital sheet-music libraries between multiple computers, from the ones that are used to scan and create the PDF files, to the devices used to receive and work with them.

When you sign up for Dropbox, you'll be given the opportunity to install the free application on your computers. Once installed, you will see Dropbox as a folder in your computer's navigation bar, just like the all-important Documents, Desktop, and other top-level folders that are the default options.

Here's the Dropbox folder on my MacBook (with my Sheet Music subfolder open):

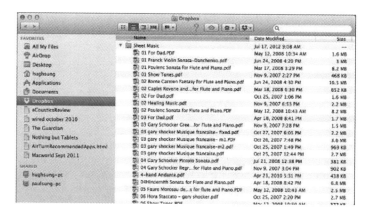

And here's what it looks like on my Windows 7 computer:

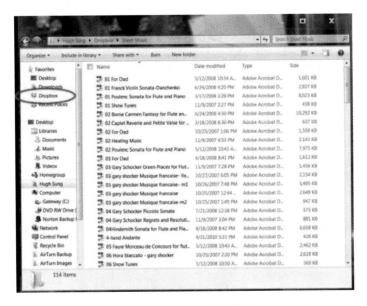

Once I scan my paper music into PDF files on my "scanning computer," I just save them within my computer's Dropbox folder (you can create subfolders within Dropbox just as easily as you would with a regular folder on your hard drive). Depending on your Internet connection speed, your files will automatically be uploaded and synchronized within your Dropbox account without any further intervention on your part.

Once your files are uploaded, you can then use your iPad to browse to your online Dropbox account, download the file, and select which app you want to open it with (see the previous chapter on opening email file attachments within your iPad's mail app – it's a similar process, but you need to make sure you are using the iPad's default Safari browser to be able to assign apps to open the file with).

Some iPad apps don't need to use Safari as an intermediary to your Dropbox files. Here are some examples of apps that can import PDF files directly from Dropbox – some have Dropbox connectivity built in, while others have their own built-in mini browsers from which you can access the web version of Dropbox:

1. forScore (Dropbox)

2. MusicPodium (Web browser)

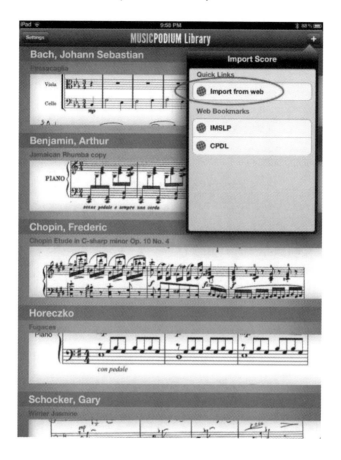

3. MusicReader PDF (Web browser)

4. OnSong (works mostly with text files, but also can work with PDFs – Dropbox)

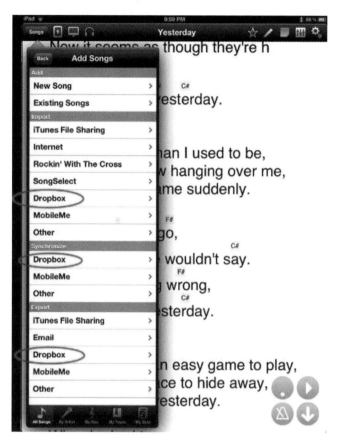

As with any wildly popular technology, imitators aren't too far behind. Apple has iCloud, Google has launched Google Drive, and Microsoft has its own SkyDrive. I haven't had a chance to play around with these newer services as much as I have Dropbox, but it might be worth adding a note of caution: any online storage service that can't pay its own bills in the long term runs the risk of suddenly disappearing one day, so be sure that you don't leave anything completely irreplaceable in the cloud. I would advise that you stick with a time-proven performer like Dropbox for the time being until these other services prove their mettle.

CHAPTER EIGHT

Transferring Converted Music to an iPad Using iTunes

Ok, so what if you don't have access to Wi-Fi or the Internet? Or what if you have a large amount of converted PDF files that you want to move in bulk from your computer to your iPad (or vice versa)? Not to worry – you can do so using the USB connector cable for your iPad and the Apple iTunes program on your Mac or PC. Check out the above picture – the iTunes icon represents your computer, and the USB cable connection you need to insert into your computer's USB port.

On most computers, the small picture of the USB symbol needs to be pointing upwards – the connector will only insert one way, so don't force it into the port, even if you're feeling particularly testy that day. The small end of the cable goes to the little hole on the bottom of your iPad, which is called the Lightning Port. (For older iPads with the 30-pin connector, look for the printed rectangle on that end of the cable, and make sure it is facing the same way as the iPad's screen before inserting it into the port.)

The now-obsolete 30-pin connector for older iPads

Most folks think of iTunes as just a media player (for music and movies), and a digital store where you can buy media files. Surprise! iTunes also works as a file-sharing service for your i-devices, giving you the ability to manually move digital files back and forth between your i-device and your computer. Of course you will need to have iTunes installed on your Mac or PC computer ahead of time, and for that you'll need to access the Internet, as Apple doesn't include installation CDs with iPads. No problem – you can download iTunes from Apple at http://www.apple.com/itunes/

You will also need to have a PDF-reading app installed on your iPad. This you can purchase through the App Store using your iPad. I'll talk more about specific apps for musicians later, but if you're looking for some quick recommendations, check out this interactive App Guide at http://airturn.com/appguide

Once iTunes is installed on your computer, it will automatically launch as soon as you connect to your iPad with the USB cable. If you don't have any music yet on your iPad, you will see this opening screen:

If you already have a music collection on your iPad, then your screen will look something like this:

In either case, look for an iPad icon along the top right tool bar and click it with your mouse to bring up the iPad window.

You should see some menu items right above the iPad window. Look for "Apps" and click on it. You will then see the following window:

Don't be fooled by the way this window looks – you can actually scroll down to another section right below, which looks something like this:

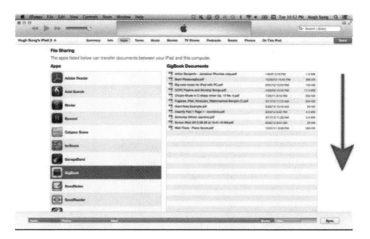

This lower portion is the "File Sharing" section. If this portion is cut off at the bottom, scroll down a teensy-weensy bit to see some additional buttons on the bottom right.

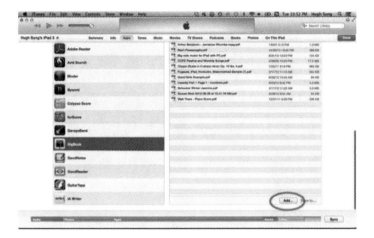

Assuming you have a PDF-reading app already installed on your iPad, scroll down the left column within the "Apps" box until you find the app that you would like to load your PDF files into. In the above example, I'm using an app called GigBook (actually short for "DeepDish GigBook"). Click on the app, and then to the immediate right you will see all the documents that are contained within that app in the window. Most likely your "Documents" window will be blank, but in any case this will be the area that shows the contents of your digital sheet-music library within that specific app.

To add your files, just click on the "Add" button on the bottom right of the "Documents" window (circled in the above picture). You will then see a navigation window pop up – in this example, I'm using a MacBook to navigate, but the Windows version will be similar. Navigate to the folder where your scanned PDF files are located. To select a single file, click on it to select it, then click on the "Open" button.

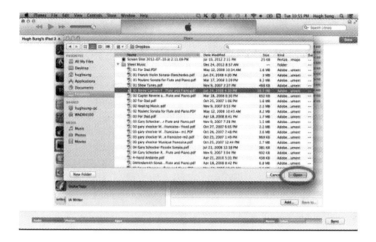

To select a group of files all at once, either drag a box to group your selections, or select the first file by clicking it, scrolling up or down to the last selection, then press and hold the "Shift" key on your keyboard while clicking the last file. You will then see all the files between the first and last selections highlighted. Click the "Open" button to move all these files into your iPad app all at once.

If you want to select a number of files but they aren't adjacent to each other, you can do so by the following combinations of keyboard key presses and mouse clicks:

- For Mac computers, press and hold the "Command ⌘" key on your keyboard, then click on the desired files with your mouse or trackpad.
- For Windows computers, press and hold the "Control" key on your keyboard, then click on the desired files with your mouse. (You'd think that after all these years one of these two companies would have given in and named the key the same. Can't we all just get along?)

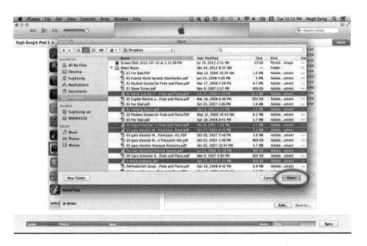

As with the previous methods, once you've finished selecting your desired files, click on the "Open" button and, poof, they are transferred to you iPad app all at once.

Conversely, if you want to copy files from your iPad to your computer, simply navigate to the "File Sharing" section as I described above, then scroll to the app that contains the files you want to move. Select the files in the "Documents" window, then click on the "Save to..." button (right next to the "Add" button on the bottom right).

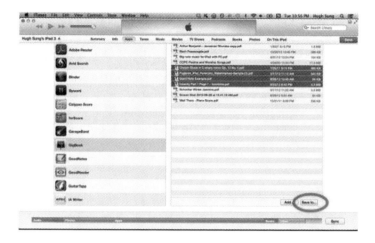

A navigation window will pop up. Navigate to the folder on your computer where you want to paste the copied files, then click on "Open."

This is a great way to copy over files in bulk all at once. By the way, you can also delete files that appear in your iPad app's "Documents" window by selecting them and pressing the "delete" key on your keyboard.

One final step before you yank that iPad off of its digital umbilical cord: DON'T PULL THE PLUG. You need to gently wean the connection between computer and iPad by first telling iTunes to eject your iPad. To do this, click on the "Done" button in the upper right hand corner:

You will then be returned to the iTunes home screen. Look for the eject icon right next to the iPad button. Click on it, and the iPad button should disappear, which means that it's safe to finally unplug your digital baby from mama computer.

Congratulations! Pat yourself on the back. You are now a master of digital juggling. Someday there may be a digital circus that needs performers who can do this while avoiding the virtual elephants in the ring. Meanwhile you can enjoy your newfound talent.

CHAPTER NINE

Transferring Digital Sheet Music to an Android Tablet

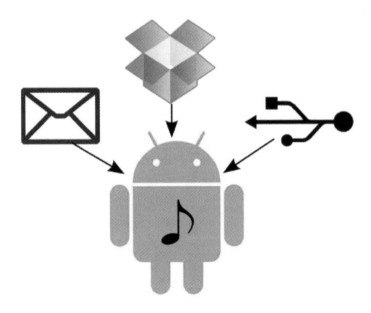

If you've spent any time with Mac or Windows PC computers, you'll be familiar with the way files are stored within folders and directories – resembling the way documents are organized in a physical office lined with filing cabinets and stuffed with file folders labeled with subject names and organized in alphabetical order – an OCD worker's dream (or nightmare) come true. Unlike Apple iPads, which try to hide those rooms full of rusting filing cabinets filled with creaking drawers stuffed with mind-numbing stacks of dog-eared file folders behind clean, shiny icons, Android tablets keep the office storage door open for you to peruse the stacks and see what a glorious mess of data you accumulate over time.

Messy as it may sound, it actually makes it easier to move files around within the Android environment, whether it's from one computer to a tablet, or as a download from the Internet. Just like we saw with the iPad, we'll look at three ways to transfer files to your Android tablet – via email, via the Internet using an online storage service like Dropbox, and via a direct USB cable connection or USB thumb drive from your computer.

As a general rule of thumb, most files sent by email attachment and downloaded from the Internet will get stored in your Android tablet's "Download" folder by default. To keep your life simple, I would recommend using the "Download" folder for USB cable transfers as well, if your tablet supports that option. Most music reading apps will have the option to navigate your Android file system to open files, and the "Download" folder should be one of the first places you look.

Transferring Files to an Android Tablet Using Email

If you weren't prompted to set up your email service with your Android tablet's mail app (or you blissfully ignored that portion of the initial setup), you can easily add your favorite service within the "Accounts" section. Either look for the settings icon, which looks like a black box with a blue border and three lines with circles set at different horizontal positions...

...or tap your task bar next to the clock and look for the sprocket wheel along the top right of the pop-up menu panel (what does a sprocket have to do with settings? I have no idea...).

Go to the "Accounts" panel (you may need to scroll down a bit to find it, depending on the tablet model you're using), then tap on "+ Add account."

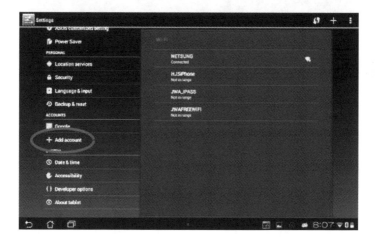

Android tablets work most easily with Google Gmail accounts (no surprise there, since Google is the proud papa of both the Android OS and Gmail services), but you can easily add a different mail account from Yahoo, Hotmail, or other service by tapping "Email" and following the prompts.

Once you've set up and synced your preferred email client, go to the home screen and look for your mail icon (It looks like an envelope. See, now THAT'S an icon that makes sense.)

Tapping on it will open all your recent email messages. From your computer, send yourself an email with your desired PDF as an attachment. On your Android tablet, tap on the mail icon and you should momentarily see that email appear with a paperclip symbol telling you that this message has something attached (your PDF file, we hope).

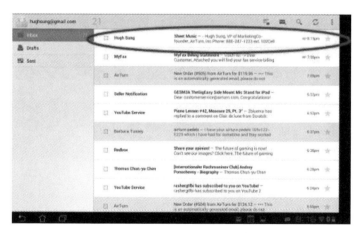

Tap on that message, then you should see something that looks like the following screenshot:

Within your opened message, you will see a header bar with "Message" and "Attachment" followed by the number of attachments in the message. Tap on the attachment section, and you will see the names of the attached files.

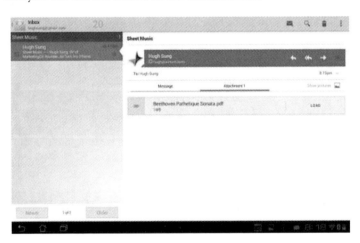

Tap on "Load," and then you will see new options appear – "View" and "Save."

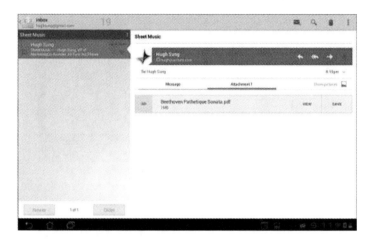

Tap on "Save," and the attachment will begin downloading. Where to? Where else? Your "Download" folder. Don't worry about following that digital puppy yet, we'll find it a good home soon enough.

Now open your favorite PDF reader app. In this example, I'm using an app called MobileSheets.

Tap on the + icon for adding files, and you should see a navigation screen appear.

Tap on the folder icon in the middle of the screen. You will automatically be taken to the "Download" folder by default, and here you will find your downloaded digital puppy. There you are, you good puppy you!

Tap on the PDF file, and a check mark will appear next to it. Tap on "Ok" at the bottom, and it will appear in the Song Editor window with a preview, where you can edit the details of the piece, such as "Title," "Artist," "Genre" and a host of other details.

Once you finish editing the details, tap "Ok" in the upper right hand corner, and the PDF file will appear in your library.

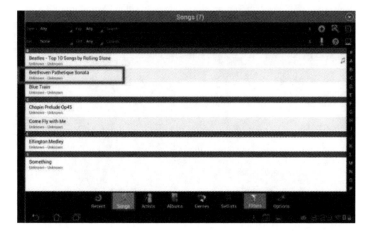

Each Android app will have its own process for adding downloaded PDF files, but essentially it will be similar: look for an icon for adding or opening a file, then look for the "Download" folder in the navigation screen or window that appears to find your desired PDF puppy.

Downloading PDF Files from Dropbox

The process for transferring files from Dropbox to your Android tablet is very similar. Instead of your mail app, use your tablet's Internet browser (the Internet browser icon usually looks like a blue globe representing the world, I suppose) and type in www.dropbox.com in the address bar.

If you don't have an account yet, you can tap on "Sign Up" to get a free 5Gig account. If you already have a Dropbox account, tap on "Sign in" below and enter your login information (if you're new to Dropbox, go back to Chapter 7 for a primer on this nifty online storage service). Ok, assuming you've finished reading Chapter 7, I'm going to assume you have PDF files uploaded into your Dropbox account. Once you've signed in and entered your login information, navigate to the file or the folder containing your PDF file.

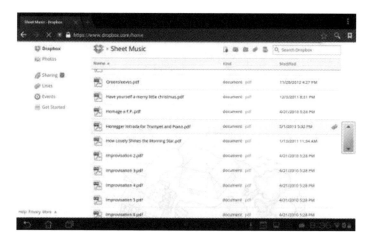

Tap on the PDF file you want to download (or the folder containing the file) – you may need to tap twice to get the file to start downloading or the folder to open, by the way. Once tapped, the file should open in your default PDF reader app.

If you don't have an app for reading PDF files, or if the one you have is a bit buggy (as is the case with the app I have on my Asus Transformer tablet), you may see an error message like this one:

Never fear, intrepid musician! Tap on "Close," then in the next screen you should see the following message:

Tap on "Save and close" and you will see the "back room" of your tablet: a column of file folders and their names. You could select any folder from this list, but I recommend tapping on the "Download" folder.

Tap on "ok" on the bottom and the file will proceed to download into that folder.

As with the email instructions above, go to your PDF reader app of choice. Tap on "Add" or "New" within the app's menu options, then you should be able to navigate to the "Download" folder to find the PDF file you just downloaded from Dropbox. Tapping on it will open that file within your app. Pretty simple, eh?

Transferring Files to an Android Tablet Using a USB Cable

Psst, wanna know a secret? That charging cable you're using for your Android tablet? Give it a pull from the block that plugs into your outlet – does it come off? If so, then you're in luck! You can probably use that cable to connect your Android tablet to your Mac or PC computer's USB port and transfer files back and forth in bulk. Go ahead and give it a try. If you see your tablet appearing as an external drive on your computer, give yourself permission to smirk smugly.

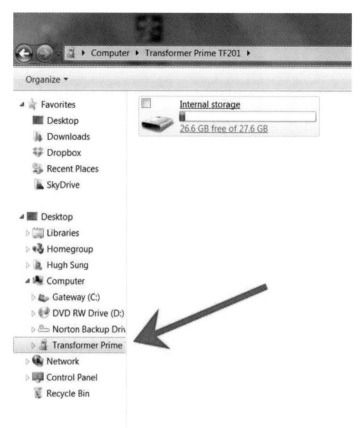

You can double click on the icon representing your tablet to enter the digital version of its file room.

You'll see lots of folders with strange names. Look for the folder named – you'll never guess – "Download." Double click the "Download" folder, and now you can drag files back and forth between your computer and your tablet. This is great for moving your entire collection all at once instead of one at a time via the email method.

As we mentioned with the iPad's USB/iTunes connection, when you're finished migrating your caravan of PDF files to its new digital digs, DON'T PULL THE PLUG. On a Mac, you'll need to right click the icon representing the tablet and select the option to "eject." On a Windows computer, go to the taskbar and look for the USB icon – right click it to select the "eject"

option. If you get an error message in Windows preventing you from ejecting your USB connection, make sure all your windows showing the contents of your tablet's file folders are closed, then try again. Windows computers can't eject an external device while there is an active folder connection. Only after the tablet icon has disappeared on the Mac screen or the Windows taskbar has given you the message that it is safe to disconnect your USB device can you physically disconnect your tablet from its USB cord.

As with the email method, open your desired PDF reader app and use the menu to navigate to the "Download" folder to open your newly transferred files.

Transferring Files to an Android Tablet Using a USB Thumb Drive

As a way of "thumbing" the iPad's aversion to USB ports, several Android tablet models come equipped with USB ports that enable you to transfer files back and forth with USB thumb drives – you know, those little metal and plastic memory stubs that love to get lost in coat pockets and backpacks? To make it easier to navigate your thumb drive's contents, use the File Manager app.

Within the File Manager app, you can copy the contents of your thumb drive into your Download folder.

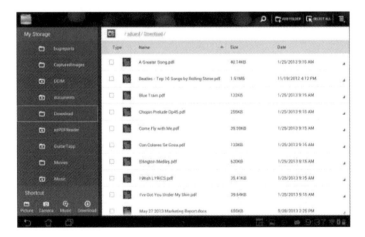

CHAPTER TEN

My Four-C Setup as a Digital Sheet-Music Musician

Ok, now I'm going to begin drilling down deep into the various kinds of equipment there is available for joining the digital sheet-music revolution. To recap a bit, I described four "Cs" that you need to get started.

They are as follows:

1. Computer
2. Content
3. Containers
4. Controllers

I asked some of my digital sheet-music-using colleagues about what they like best, but I thought I'd start the ball rolling by sharing what my own four Cs entail.

What I Do as a Musician

I'm a collaborative classical pianist (polite-speak for "accompanist," or "someone who plays nice with others"). I perform with all sorts of musicians, mainly instrumentalists. I work with flute players, violinists, violists, and just about any other instrumentalist that you would find in a classical symphony orchestra (and then some). I've played in lots of places around the world and have made a number of recordings, several of which you'll find on iTunes, Amazon and other online music resources. I also work with orchestras mainly accompanying private rehearsals between the conductor and visiting soloists, but also accompanying for job auditions, and sometimes even playing as part of the orchestra.

Why I Switched to Digital Sheet Music

Because I play with so many different kinds of instrumentalists, I work with an enormous repertoire of music. I always struggled with having all the music I needed on hand, and carrying everything I need for a tour or even a full day of rehearsals would be a major pain in the ... shoulder. I also have a terrible habit of forgetting things – car keys, children, business cards and, of course, paper music. I wanted to find a way to be able to carry my entire library with me everywhere I went, easily and without being a pain in the ... brain. Being able to call up any piece instantly was another huge benefit I saw from switching to digital music.

My Four Cs

1. Computer

I actually use a number of computers, depending on the task at hand. For the vast majority of rehearsals, recordings, and live performances, I use an **iPad 4** (the "new" iPad, as Apple likes to call it). I like its portability and relatively good battery life (although you need to keep the iPad 4's screen brightness at 50 percent, keep Wi-Fi turned off when you're not actively using it, blah blah – but I digress. I'll get into all those nitty-gritty details later).

I get asked to write arrangements from time to time, so for that I use a **MacBook Pro** (having been a longtime steadfast Windows champion, I can hear my Mac friends cheering now). If I have access to my grand piano at home, I can hook up to it via a MIDI interface to write my music (my piano has a MIDI strip installed. Very cool to be able to play an acoustic instrument and get a digital output! Thanks, Cunningham Piano!)

I used to teach a number of private students, and still get asked for a private lesson here and there from both younger students and professional colleagues (yes, professional musicians get lessons from each other – it's a cool thing when you're open-minded enough to keep learning!). For those lessons, I tend to use a **Lenovo X200 Tablet PC**. It's an older machine, but I really love the way I can draw my annotations on the music naturally with the digital pen. I sync my Tablet PC up with my iPad via Wi-Fi to show my Tablet PC's screen on my iPad using a neat application called <u>Splashtop</u>. That way I can keep my iPad next to the student on the piano music rack and stay seated in a position where I can observe the student without having to constantly get up and down to show what I'm talking about on the music – the student sees the markings I'm making on the music right on the iPad. Cool, eh? (Or am I being too nerdy for you?)

2. Content

Since most of my music is made up of classical music in the public domain, I use a website called the **International Music Score Library Project** – <u>www.imslp.org</u> – to get most of what I need. The sheet music is completely free, and downloads as PDF files.

Occasionally, I won't be able to find something on IMSLP. My second go-to site for classical sheet music is <u>www.EveryNote.com</u>. This is a commercial site so I have to buy my music there, but the prices are very reasonable and the sheet music also downloads as PDF files.

To read music on my iPad, I use an app called <u>**forScore**</u>. This is a full-featured PDF reader. I can mark up the music in different colored inks and highlights, rearrange the pages in any order, and even create PDF files from photos taken from my iPad 4's built-in camera, or from photos I've emailed to myself from my iPhone 4S.

Another iPad app I regularly use to read music is **DeepDish GigBook**. I work from a large 300+ page PDF file for playing music at church. Rather than having to flip through the pages to find the hymn I need, I use DeepDish GigBook's Super Bookmarking feature to extract each song as if it were a standalone file. Making set lists for Sunday worship is a breeze thanks to these Super Bookmarks.

If I find myself teaching without my Tablet PC, I'll use **MusicReader PDF** on my iPad. I find the ink marking a bit easier and faster with MusicReader PDF, particularly if I'm turning pages hands-free at the same time (more on that later).

If I need to get access to more popular music (Broadway

tunes, jazz favorites, movies music, etc.), I use a website called Musicnotes.com. Musicnotes has a free iPad sheet-music viewing app. The first time I logged into the app with my Musicnotes.com account information, I was pleasantly surprised to find that every single piece of sheet music I had purchased from them (and subsequently lost) over the years instantly appeared in the app! Now all my sheet music is truly "unforgettable"!

To read music on my MacBook Pro, I use a program called **MusicReader PDF 4**. This is different from the iPad version, made by the same developer. While the iPad app is just a PDF viewer (with the ability to mark up the music in colored inks), the Mac/PC version of MusicReader PDF 4 has a lot more features for not only viewing and marking up your music, but also for creating PDF files from scratch using scanned or downloaded images as sources. Remember the size-12 feet and size-7 shoe illustration? MusicReader PDF 4 does a really good job of making awkward things fit by utilizing a variety of screen-viewing options.

For my MacBook Pro laptop, I use MusicReader PDF 4's half-screen viewing option. This allows me to see the top half of a page, then the bottom half, then the top half of the next page, etc. so that I don't have to squint at teeny tiny notes squished the wrong way on my horizontal screen. You can even adjust where the half page breaks so that you aren't cutting off an important piece of music between page turns. There are a bunch of other neat tools that come with the program, which I'll cover in more detail in a coming chapter.

To teach with music on my Lenovo Tablet PC, I use both MusicReader PDF 4 and another PDF program called **PDF Annotator**. I absolutely love the smooth inking quality with PDF Annotator, which makes it a great teaching tool. Page turns can be a bit slow, and there's no way to create set lists/playlists (a feature I use regularly with MusicReader PDF 4 for recitals), so I don't use PDF Annotator for performances.

3. Containers

Since 99 percent of the time I'm working with acoustic grand pianos that have built-in music racks, I don't really need a container. However, on occasion, I do run across a piano with a broken or missing music rack. In those instances, I pop my iPad out of my **Adonit Writer Plus** Bluetooth keyboard case and set it within the frame so that the music is vertical. The Adonit Writer Plus case has magnets in the cover that can secure the keyboard in almost any angle, making it pretty flexible as an ad hoc iPad music stand for my needs.

*Using my Adonit Writer Plus iPad case
as an ad hoc music stand*

Thanks to a tip from Christopher O'Riley (host of "From The Top", a popular classical music radio and TV show for kids), I've recently started using a nifty new tablet holder that allows me to take the piano rack off and give a cool look to my digital sheet music reader. The Compass works as a svelte aluminum tripod that folds up into a unit small enough to fit in my pocket.

Compass Mobile Stand by Twelve South

Despite its minimalist size and design, the Compass is surprisingly sturdy, even while banging the loudest portions of Rachmaninoff's "Rhapsody on a Theme of Paganini" with Orchestra.

Views of my Compass supporting my iPad on a concert grand piano

While the Compass is primarily designed for iPads, I could see this working for a large number of other similar sized tablets.

In the past, I've also used a case from Targus, which had the ability to rotate the iPad for both horizontal and vertical views.

A Targus case for the iPad featuring a nifty rotate feature

4. Controllers

I used to teach video lessons using a laptop connected to a large monitor. To mark up the music, I used a digital drawing pad called the **Bamboo Tablet**, made by Wacom. The Bamboo Tablet would connect to my laptop via a USB cord, and allow me to use a digital pen like a mouse. It took a little getting used to drawing with my eyes on the screen and my hand in another place, but if you can get used to working with a computer mouse, after some practice you'll have no problem adjusting to one of these pen tablets.

Teaching video lessons with my computers and a Wacom Bamboo Tablet

An older Bamboo digital drawing tablet

The newer Wacom Bamboo Tablets feature both pen and touch control (meaning that you can use the pen as a mouse and slide your fingers on the tablet surface like a giant laptop trackpad).

A newer Bamboo drawing tablet for pen and touchpad control

For turning pages while reading my digital sheet music, I use a wireless page-turning pedal called an **AirTurn**. Since my right foot controls the damper pedal, the one that lets the strings ring and sustain their sound after the piano key hammer hits them, I use my left foot to control the AirTurn pedal. This allows me to keep my hands on the piano at all times. Sweet Freedom! I no longer need to interrupt my playing with a finger to tap a button on my computer or swipe the screen on my iPad to turn the page.

The AirTurn BT-105 Bluetooth pedal will work with any tablet or computer that can connect to a Bluetooth keyboard. The AirTurn AT-104 is a wireless USB version that works with any computer that can use a USB keyboard. For both models, one pedal turns pages forwards and the other pedal turns pages backwards, easy-peasy. More on this later.

The AirTurn BT-105 Bluetooth page-turning pedal

AirTurn AT-104 wireless USB page turning pedal

Now I'm going to turn to some of my esteemed colleagues who have become digital-sheet-music enthusiasts, and share what made them decide to join the revolution, what they are using, and so on.

CHAPTER ELEVEN

Steve Hoover: Multi-Musician and His Four-C Digital Sheet-Music Setup

When I was a youngster, I dabbled with a bunch of different instruments. I tried my hand at playing a little guitar, fooled around with the harmonica, took some lessons on the French horn, and even studied the violin semi-seriously for a few years. Frankly, I stuck with the piano because it was the easiest instrument for me to make a decent sound with, and I was super lazy about practicing. So when a one-trick pony like me hears about a multifaceted musician like **Steve Hoover**, my envy streak makes Kermit the Frog look like an albino gecko! Here's a guy who can do EVERYTHING – he plays the keyboards, bass, trombone, tuba, and he even sings, for crying out loud! And that's just the performing side of his talents!

Here's a look at Steve Hoover and his four-C setup for being a digital sheet-music musician.

* * *

1. What do you do as a musician?

I have a degree in Music Ed. from SIU-Edwardsville, and I taught music in MO public schools (University City & Ritenour) for 17 years prior to becoming a full-time musician 14 years ago. I am the keyboardist/ bassist/MD for the **Bob Kuban Band** in St. Louis (bobkuban.com), and I play keys/bass in a PW band at First Christian Church in my hometown of Edwardsville, IL. And I have my all-Beatles-all-the-time project, **The Abbey Road Warriors** (abbeyroadwarriors.com). I play bass, keyboard, trombone and sing in that group. I play occasional brass quintet gigs on trombone or tuba. I also write and arrange music for other artist/bands – I'm an avid user of Sibelius – and I have access to a project-recording studio.

2. Why did you switch from paper to digital sheet music?

The convenience factor is huge! And being able to turn pages hands-free with **AirTurn** makes performance so much easier and less stressful. Sometimes it's tough to get a hand free to physically turn a paper page. AirTurn eliminates that hassle. I keep all the music for my performing groups on my iPad, as well as a large library of fake books to cover requests that come up. I also don't need a music-stand light when using the iPad since it provides its own illumination. I've been using **DeepDish GigBook,** and I'm very happy with it – it does everything I need and in an elegant and logical way.

3. What are your four "Cs"?

– Computer (for reading music)?
iPad 2

– Content (what kind of music do you read and where do you get it)?
I create my own PDFs from charts I do in Sibelius (*a very popular music notation program for Mac and PC computers*). I also scan music to PDF. I sometimes purchase music from Musicnotes.com, as well.

– Container (do you use any special holders for your computer)?
I use **TheGigEasy.** It's been awesome. I can place the iPad at the optimum spot and it stays put.

117

Steve uses TheGigEasy to turn his iPad 2
into a digital sheet-music stand

– Controller (Do you use any special controllers for reading or working with your digital sheet music)?

I use the **AirTurn** (*a wireless page-turning pedal for the iPad*). Wow, is this thing well built! I have used it 3-4 times a week since I got it on everything from hardwood to carpet and concrete, and it still looks fantastic! And I step on it repeatedly! It has never let me down and has always worked the way it should.

Steve Hoover and the Abbey Road Warriors Band

CHAPTER TWELVE

Bob Bell: A Better Page Turner for Organists

For some musicians who need to use both hands – and both feet – to play their instruments, something as simple as turning pages for sheet music can pose considerable challenges. Organists, harpists, and drummers are some examples of musicians who have both hands and both feet constantly in use.

Bob Bell, founder of <u>BCSTech, LLC</u>, and organist for his local church, has developed "<u>One Good Turn</u>," a custom computer system for reading music, which includes an ingenious way for musicians to turn pages – hands AND feet free. Here's a 4-C look at Bob's digital sheet-music setup and unique page-turning solution, the idea for which quite literally "fell out of the sky!"

– Computer

Bob Bell's "One Good Turn" system consists of a customized 21-inch touchscreen Windows 7 computer loaded with <u>MusicReader PDF 4</u>. The screen is large enough to display two full-sized pages at a time, yet weighs only 8 pounds and can be carried with the help of a carrying case.

– Content

Bob uses scanned PDF files of his hymnal as well as other miscellaneous choral and organ solo works. As mentioned above, the MusicReader PDF 4 software not only enables him to view his music digitally, but he can also use the software to organize, catalog, and instantly pull up any piece he needs to find, as well as create playlists/setlists for each worship service from his digital library. MusicReader PDF 4 also gives him the ability to mark up his music with color ink and highlights, using his finger to "draw" directly on the Windows-based touchscreen computer (no need to fumble around for blunt pencils or worn-out erasers).

Although a 21-inch screen is large enough to display two full-sized pages at a time, if necessary, he can also set MusicReader's viewing option to half a page a time, zooming the music dramatically. This can be a terrific solution for low-vision musicians, not just organists. We'll talk more about solutions for low-vision musicians in a later chapter.

By the way, if you're looking for a way to have someone *else* scan your hymnal into a PDF file, BCSTech provides document-scanning services ($2 per page at the time of this writing with a 10-page minimum – resulting scanned files will be emailed to the customer, ready to be loaded onto the One Good Turn system).

– Container

As each organ design is unique, Bob offers custom-made brackets to secure his One Good Turn system safely onto any organ music rack.

– Controller

The Windows touchscreen computer eliminates the need for any additional pen input devices (although I suppose a soft rubber stylus could be used if drawing with fingers brings back queasy memories of messy smocks from kindergarten).

And now, drum roll please – Ladies and Gentlemen, the "unique page-turning solution" you've been probably skipping down the page to discover:

A *bite switch* connected to an AirTurn AT-104 wireless USB digital page turner.

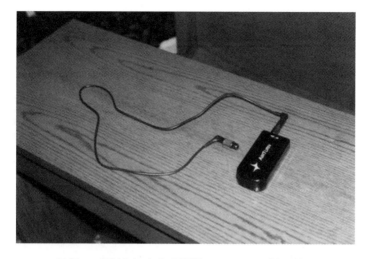

AirTurn AT-104 wireless USB page turner with a bite switch

The bite switch was originally designed for skydivers who want to be able to take pictures while plummeting to the earth. Since their hands are flopping and flailing uselessly while they are being buffeted by high-velocity air, the bite switch enables them to trigger digital cameras mounted on their helmets hands free. I never knew that Bob was into skydiving, but thanks to his out-of-the-box (or "out-of-the-plane?") thinking, he's been able to adapt this bite switch to trigger digital page turns via the AirTurn AT-104 instead of a pedal or foot switch.

The AirTurn AT-104 itself consists of a wireless transmitter nestled in a shirt or pants pocket, and a USB receiver that plugs into the Windows 7 computer. Biting the switch triggers the AT-104 to send a Page Down (PgDn) keyboard command to turn the digital page.

Some might think this sounds pretty far-fetched (a polite way of saying "gross"), or might wonder how visually intrusive such an approach might be. I'll let you be the judge of that:

The AT-104 transmitter rests in Bob's shirt pocket. The switch requires a firm bite, but since the human jaw is the strongest muscle, it's surprisingly easy. The switch itself is curved in such a way that it rests in the mouth with no danger of being swallowed (and there's a cable to yank the pesky switch out of your esophagus in case the unthinkable happens). And the action is so subtle no one can see how the pages are being turned.

Here's another look at the One Good Turn computer system with MusicReader PDF 4 displaying two pages of music and the AirTurn AT-104 with bite switch:

You can see Bob Bell demonstrating his system here: http://www.youtube.com/watch?v=PU0deGXTJpM?rel=0

CHAPTER THIRTEEN

Sharyn Byer: A Forward-Looking Flutist

There! I've resolved that silly contention between the words "flautist" and "flutist" once and for all! A guitarist plays the guitar, an organist plays the organ, and a flutist plays the flute. It simply doesn't make sense to think of a "flautist" playing a "flaut," does it? You may disagree with me if you are on the other side of the pond we call the Atlantic Ocean, but for right now I'm putting my etymological foot down and sticking to my flutes!

Sharyn Byer is another example of a forward-looking musician who enjoys a very active performing and touring life. Here's a look at Sharyn's 4-C setup for her digital sheet-music needs.

* * *

What do you do as a musician?

I graduated from the University of Miami School of Music and am Principle Flute of The Capital City Symphony in Washington, D.C. I teach at Columbia Institute of Fine Arts and direct The Columbia Flute Choir (www.columbiaflutechoir.org). I tour with the International Flute Orchestra, and have performed in Europe, Russia, China and South America. I also play in First Light Ensemble and have performed locally in the D.C. area including at The White House.

Why did you switch from paper to digital sheet music?

I love having all my music available on one device, my iPad, and being able to easily take it all with me when I travel. Page turns are no problem with the AirTurn Bluetooth foot pedals! I can keep both hands on my flute at all times!! Dark stages are not a problem, either. I don't even need a stand light because the scores are backlit on the iPad! Also, I don't feel like I'm hiding behind a big music stand because the iPad is so small. I can even position the music as close to me as I want and still see the conductor or the audience!

What are your "4-C's"?

– Computer (for reading music)?

The iPad 2

– Content (what kind of music do you read and where do you get it from)?

I scan music into my computer and transfer to the forScore app on my iPad through iTunes. I can also open emailed PDFs with the forScore app. Once in forScore, I can store music by title, composer, genre, or keyword. I can even annotate the music and create setlists for different ensembles or performances.

– Container (do you use any special holders for your computer)?

I have two holders that I like. The Gig Easy Mic Stand Mount is very secure and sturdy. I also like the CrisKenna Xclip, which is actually the one I travel with because it is less bulky. When I play C flute in First Light Ensemble, I am seated and use the iPad holder on a Mic Stand Concertino. When I play in a symphony orchestra, I use the Mic Stand Concertino with a gooseneck extension because I need the iPad a little higher so I can also see the conductor. When I play the Contrabass flute, I need to stand to play so I use both the 13" and the 6" goosenecks on the Concertino stand and that works great! I can fit the Concertino and both goosenecks in one of my old folding music stand cloth cases, and it goes easily in my gig bag. That's what I used in Croatia when I played with the International Flute Orchestra! If I am playing locally, I can also just use a mic stand but that won't fit in a carry-on bag for flying!

The GigEasy and iPad vs. the Music Stand

‒ Controller (do you use any special controllers for reading or working with your digital sheet music)?

I use the AirTurn BT-105 Bluetooth transceiver and two ATSF-2 foot switches for hands-free page turning (I need to keep both hands on my flute.) It works great on any floor surface, and I am amazed how long the charge lasts. It is so easy to recharge with the iPad charger, even overseas!

- Sharyn Byer, sharyn@flute.pro

Sharyn Byer and the Columbia Flute Choir at The White House

CHAPTER FOURTEEN

Caleb Overstreet: How to Conduct a Digital Revolution

Caleb Overstreet graduated from Baylor University in Texas in May, 2013 with a Bachelors of Vocal Music Education in May 2013. I had the opportunity to meet Caleb at the 2012 TMEA (Texas Music Educators Association) Convention in San Antonio, where he, in turn, had his first exposure to the possibilities of reading and working with sheet music digitally. I will never forget the "saucer eyes of wonder" on Caleb's face! Very soon afterward, Caleb dove headlong into the world of digital sheet music. Here's his perspective on this new technological – and musical – journey.

* * *

First and foremost, I am a singer. Additionally I play the piano and guitar. I am a member of a handful of choirs at school, two of which tour regionally and nationally. Apart from school, I lead worship at my church, and play at special occasions such as weddings. Within the next few years, hopefully, I will be a choir director at a Texas public high school.

The decision to switch from paper to digital sheet music was more of a mental decision and desire to change long before I actually was able, due to the strain and rigor of both being in college and working. I switched, however, because of the convenience and longevity of digital music. Anytime I have my iPad, I always have my entire choral library, all my worship songs, and any other music with me. In just the few months I have had my music digitized, I cannot count the number of times that I have benefited from the convenience!

– Computer

I use a combination of things along with my digitized music. To transfer files from my hard drive to my iPad, I use my 64GB 4G+WIFI Apple iPad in addition to my old and aging Toshiba Satellite laptop. I also continue to expand my digital library, so I plan on getting an external hard drive to store the original files. That way I can have everything backed up just in case something were to happen to my iPad.

− Content

I have an ever-increasing amount of full choral scores, a handful of full orchestral scores, about 30 or so voice and piano solos, along with a hundred plus chord charts − all of which is slowly increasing. I get this music from various places. Most of it I scanned myself, but I am beginning to use digital downloads from various online sources.

− Container

I don't have any particular case for my iPad, simply because it stays in my backpack or briefcase as I go to rehearsals or performances. However, while I am playing worship, I have gotten quite a bit of use out of **TheGigEasy** − a mount custom built for the iPad that clamps on the side, or can be attached to the top of, a normal mic stand. It makes performing in smaller spaces very convenient, and I have even come to prefer it to the much larger music stand. After all, when it is attached to the side of a mic stand, it makes for one less music stand clogging up the stage.

− Controller

Lastly, I make great use of the **AirTurn BT-105 foot pedal**, particularly for turning pages while playing or conducting. Heads certainly turn when they realize that I am not turning pages while I am conducting off of my iPad, which turns enough heads by itself. People are even more impressed when I show them how convenient it is with the AirTurn pedal system. Additionally, it works perfectly in the worship setting. There are times when I need to look ahead for seamless transitions from one song to the next, which I can do without having to stop playing to turn the page with my hand. I simply tap the pedal with my foot without having to stop playing. Also, there are times when I want to go back and repeat the chorus of a previous song. Then I simply tap the back pedal and it turns back the page! I truly cannot express to you how amazing and seamless this one pedal makes playing and conducting!

Caleb conducting from his iPad and turning pages hands free with an AirTurn

I am very grateful for all the people who helped me along the path, and who make this transition possible for me. I look forward to continuing my musical career as a pioneer to the digital-music world, and am excited about where it is heading!

CHAPTER FIFTEEN

Janette McIntyre: Computerized Cruise-Ship Cocktail Pianist

If you've ever had the chance to relax to the sounds of a live piano played by a human pianist while dining at a nice restaurant, you know what a magical experience it can be, especially compared to the dreadful music piped in over a speaker system.

A good cocktail pianist is the epitome of cool, a musical sommelier that serves up aural delicacies tickled on ivories. For all my 40 years of experience playing the piano, I find the role of cocktail pianist to be far more intimidating than stepping out on stage at Carnegie Hall due to one deceptively portentous word: "request." The better-armed cocktail pianists are loaded down with stacks of fake books, and overstuffed binders bulge from beneath the piano or are splayed haphazardly over the music rack. How they know even where to begin to look for that obscure tune is a marvel of real-time information management.

Janette McIntyre provides a fascinating behind-the-scenes look at the life of a cocktail pianist on a cruise ship, and how she managed to evolve her work into a true "dream job," thanks to her use of technology.

* * *

My passion is playing the piano. After having a career as an administrator and executive, I decided that playing the piano on a cruise ship would be just the permanent vacation from life I'd been looking for! Play the piano a few hours a day, cruise and lay in the sun in the balmy Caribbean the rest of the time. So, on a whim, I joined the ranks of the entertainers for Carnival Cruise Line.

For the first five years I struggled with literally pounds of sheet music that I rolled up like scrolls so I didn't have to turn pages. They were even taped together. As one might imagine, the system was not good. There really was no system. Even when a song was requested that I knew I had in my "bag," it wasn't easy to find.

After one contract in 2011, I had enough of the lack of organization. I knew that there was a better way, and had actually talked about "inventing" something that could turn the page on the computer. One of the musicians told me about a device that would do just that, and we actually looked it up on line while on the ship. I was sold.

I changed my computer from a PC to a MacBook Pro, and bought myself an iPad. All of my music was scanned – thousands of sheets of my own sheet music and books – and then transferred to the iPad using the **NextPage** app. The purchase of the **AirTurn BT-105** page-turning pedal completed the hardware setup. I was ready to go.

The first day back on the ship was a little tense. No paper sheet music, and blind faith (again) that all would work as planned. It did! I've never looked back. The only hair-raising day was when I forgot to recharge the iPad and it came up with a "low battery" indication half way through a set. Yikes! I hurried through the set, went downstairs to give it a quick 15-, or maybe 20-minute, battery charge, and finished the night.

On the ship many people enjoy the relaxing piano music, and often they are watching my fingers. Standing behind me and seeing just the iPad and no sheet music has fascinated many. They ask how it's done and how I turn the pages. Sometimes I joke and tell them that I blow on it! They actually believe me, and I laugh and tell them the truth. I received so many inquiries that I printed business cards praising not only the iPad but the AirTurn and Next Page app, as well. I also include my email address so people can ask me questions once they are back home.

As a musician who doesn't want to use up much-needed brain cells to memorize ANYTHING, I always had a hard time just sitting down without music and playing the piano when asked. No one carries their music everywhere they go. Now it's rare that I leave home without the iPad and AirTurn, which fit right into my small briefcase-like carrier. I can play anywhere and, with the NextPage app, I can instantly pull up any requested song.

CHAPTER SIXTEEN

How to Select the Perfect Computer for Reading Digital Sheet Music, Part 1

Years ago, when I still had a beautiful wood-paneled office at The Curtis Institute of Music, I received a phone call from a MusicPad Pro sales rep. She wanted to stop by for an in-person demonstration of their digital music-reading device, and was willing to take the train all the way from Washington D.C. to Philadelphia to do so.

A few days later, she was in my office waxing poetic about all the amazing things the MusicPad Pro could do for a professional musician like me, and proceeded to dig in her roller bag and pull out a rather bulky slate. It took forever for the unit to boot up, giving the sales rep plenty of opportunity to try to fill the awkward silence with techie talk.

The display was rather dim, and she tried to demonstrate the touchscreen annotation features, but the pesky screen wasn't being very cooperative. It took several jabs of the plastic stylus to try to get a stubborn line of digital ink to appear. After several minutes of her fumbling with the device and apologizing for its reticent performance, I pulled out my own system: a slender Fujitsu Stylistic 5032D slate tablet PC. For the same $1,000 MusicPad Pro price tag, I had a digital pen with the responsiveness of a Mont Blanc pen, and the ability to not only read sheet-music files, but also run music notation programs like Finale and Sibelius, as well as full versions of Microsoft Office and any other Windows XP program I wanted to load up. Even more embarrassing was the fact that the MusicPad Pro didn't have any internal memory to speak of – you had to rely on memory cards to store your files, whereas my tablet PC had a whopping 40-gig hard drive, which was more than enough space for all my programs, as well as my entire library of PDF sheet-music files.

The sales rep sheepishly admitted she really didn't have an ice-cube's chance in Miami when it came to comparing the two systems. And while both the MusicPad Pro and my beloved Fujitsu Stylistic Tablet PC have long-since been discontinued, I've been able to migrate all the PDF files I had stored on that old machine into my 4th-generation iPad, whereas the proprietary file formats that were strictly limited to the MusicPad Pro have died with that device, leaving a whole slew of customers in techno-purgatory.

Over the 12 years that I've been a "paperless pianist," I've worked with a wide range of computers for my digital sheet-music-reading needs. Computer technologies have come and gone, but the overall improvements have been staggering. Despite the rapid pace of change, the good news is that if you know what to look for, you really don't have to worry about keeping up with bleeding-edge devices as much as you might think. Your digital sheet-music library – if it's set up with longevity in mind – will far outlast any of the devices used to store and read them.

Case in point: I'm still using PDF files that I created 12 years ago. So, rather than recommending particular computer brand names or specific models, in the following chapters I'll share some general principles to help you make confident decisions about the best computer for your digital sheet-music-reading needs.

CHAPTER SEVENTEEN

Selecting the Perfect Computer for Reading Your Sheet Music: Three Key Questions

In your search for the perfect sheet-music-reading computer, rather than getting hung up on mumbo jumbo techno terms or micro-analyzing system specifications, you need to ask just three basic questions:

- What do you want to do (besides become famous and make a million bucks)?
- Where do you want to go (besides a beach in Croatia)?
- What do you want to see (No, not that!)?

First, *what do you want to do* (this really is a question about sheet music)*?*

Most computers and tablets will give you the basic ability to read PDF and text files, but what if you want to be able to mark up your music with annotations? What if you want to create set lists, or transpose your music into any key? What if you want to project your music onto a larger screen for a classroom or auditorium, or simply want to be able to turn pages hands free?

Your search, therefore, must begin with the applications, or "apps," for tablets. Any given computer or tablet can have the fastest processor or the best whiz-bang display specs, but if it doesn't have the ability to run an application that does what you want it to do, then it's just a shiny (and very expensive) paperweight. Conversely, if you search for the cheapest computer without considering the applications that can run on it, then you'll simply have a cheaper (and slower) paperweight. Ever see those old Mac cubes that people have turned into aquariums? You get the idea.

Several months ago, a friend of mine was eager to show off an HP TouchPad that he managed to buy on eBay for only $100. The problem was that he didn't realize that Hewlett-Packard discontinued this cool little tablet only 49 days after its launch, and that its webOS operating system had virtually no programs available for it outside of the ones bundled with the unit. The HP TouchPad featured great design, slick performance and a price that couldn't be beat, but it was absolutely worthless as a digital sheet-music reader (or much else, for that matter. You couldn't even turn it into an aquarium). And remember that

MusicPad Pro? It was powered by a proprietary version of Linux running essentially a single program. The MusicPad Pro suffered from price, choked from closed systems, and died a pitiful death by design.

The first place to begin to understand your computer choices is to look at the major operating systems – OS for short – that bring computers to life and give them the ability to perform any given task. Despite the dizzying array of computers, laptops and tablets on the market, currently there are only *three* major players in the computer OS arena powering devices large enough for reading sheet music:

1. Microsoft
2. Apple
3. Google

Microsoft, Apple, and Google

Each of these players provides a number of operating systems for a variety of computer/tablet devices. Here's a rough breakdown:

I. Microsoft

A. OS for computers
- Windows (XP, Vista, 7, 8)

B. OS for tablets
- Surface RT (Window's lame attempt at creating an operating system for tablets. My advice? Avoid this. It's a dud.)
- Surface Pro (It's a full version of Windows 8 that is flexible enough to run on tablets that are more expensive. Between (cough-

cough ... lame) Surface RT and (FTW=for the win=pretty darn good) Surface Pro, it's a no-brainer which you can opt for if you have your heart set on staying within the Windows ecosphere.

II. Apple
A. OS for computers
- OS X (Leopard, Snow Leopard, Mountain Lion, Lion)

B. OS for tablets
- iOS (for iPad, iPhone, and iPod Touch devices)

III. Google
A. Android for tablets (Honeycomb, Ice Cream Sandwich, Jelly Bean ... more yummy dessert flavors sure to come)

B. Chrome for computers. This is an unusual operating system designed to only run applications that reside on the web, so you'll need to have continuous access to the Internet. Probably not the best operating system to use on a stage with spotty WiFi access...

The basic thing to understand is that an application written for one OS generally will not work on any other OS platform (there are special exceptions with Apple emulators for running Windows programs, and even some Windows emulators on iPads, but that's a bit beyond the scope of this book). You'll sometimes find multiple versions of an application available for different operating systems, particularly between Microsoft Windows and Apple OS X computers (**Adobe Acrobat Reader** and **MusicReader PDF 4** are examples of PDF-reading programs that run on both operating systems), but you will search a long time for cross-OS versions of sheet-music-reading apps for tablets.

So the takeaway lesson is this:
IGNORE THE BLING AND START WITH THE APP.

I will explore specific apps in the "Content" sections beginning with chapter 22, but first let's consider the possibilities.

CHAPTER EIGHTEEN

Selecting the Perfect Computer for Reading Sheet Music, Mobile & Stationary Options

After considering what you want to be able to do, and determining the best operating system and apps to perform those tasks, the next question is, ***where do you want to go?*** This has to do with your need for – or lack of – mobility as a musician. Are you a gigging musician constantly traveling to a variety of venues, that Croatian beach, for example? Or are you a stationary musician performing or teaching from a single fixed location? Perhaps you're a mix of mobile and stationary and need a variety of digital sheet-music options to accommodate each situation. Whatever the case, start by examining what to look for in mobile and stationary computers, as well as some interesting hybrid solutions.

Mobile Computers

While laptop computers have been in existence since the early 1980s, and Microsoft's tablet PCs have been around since 2001, it was Apple's re-envisioning of the tablet computer as the iPad that revolutionized the idea of using computers to read digital sheet music. Even though I said I didn't want to mention specific brands or models, it's impossible to overlook the iPad's impact. This mobile computer is incredibly portable, turns on instantly, is easy to use, and features a full-day battery.

There *are* other options, particularly if you need a larger screen for viewing your music while still being able to carry your computer around. For example, you can find tablet PCs in both convertible and slate versions that run full versions of the Windows OS. Android tablets from a wide variety of manufacturers have invaded the market, offering cheaper alternatives to the iPad and, in some cases, larger screens. And there's nothing wrong with simply using a laptop if you can work with vertical music on a horizontal screen (more about laptop/desktop software options in the "Content" section, as well as some interesting solutions for mounting your laptop as a music stand in the "Containers" section). And with Ultrabooks offering a much slimmer and lighter version of the laptop form factor, with battery life rivaling the best tablets, your options are wide indeed.

Here is a simple comparison grid of features for tablets, tablet PCs, laptops and Ultrabooks:

	Tablets	Tablet PCs	Laptops	Ultrabooks
Operating Systems	iOS / Android/Windows (RT & 8)	Windows	Windows / Mac OS X	Windows / Mac OS X
Screen size	Smaller than paper (8.5"x11")	Paper Size (8.5"x11") and a bit larger	Paper size and larger available	Paper size available
Bulk/Weight	Super Light to Light	Medium to Heavy	Medium to Heavy	Light to Medium
Viewing options	Vertical and Horizontal	Vertical and Horizontal	Horizontal	Horizontal
Input options	Finger, stylus	Keyboard*, mouse, finger*, digital pen	Keyboard, mouse, external digital pen, finger*	Keyboard, mouse, external digital pen, finger*
Memory	Small to medium	Medium to large	Large	Medium to Large
Battery life	Moderate to Long	Short to Moderate	Short to Moderate	Moderate to Long
Price	$ to $$	$$$	$ to $$$	$$ to $$$

*only available with certain models

Stationary Computers

If you are a stationary musician – an organist, say – then you may want to look for a stationary-computer solution. Traditional desktop computers are made up of several components:

- The computer itself (the box "brain")
- The monitor (what you use to look at the information coming from the computer)
- Input devices (what you use to enter information, most typically a keyboard and a mouse)

At the very least, you'll need to deal with the cable to connect your monitor to your computer and, unless you get wireless versions, cables to connect your keyboard and mouse, as well. If you don't want to deal with the equipment and cable clutter typically associated with traditional desktop computers, then consider an all-in-one computer, which integrates a touchscreen monitor and the computer itself into a single unit. Instead of using a mouse, you can touch and move things directly on the screen with your finger.

This comes in very handy when you want to draw digital-ink annotations on your music, or scribble a nasty margin note to the long-dead composer. You also can call up a virtual keyboard and type text right on the screen. Keep in mind that, as of this writing, touchscreen all-in-one computers are only available for Windows operating systems.

An "All-In-One" computer from HP

Desktop computers give you the option to use very large monitors to super-size the view of your digital sheet music. Touchscreen all-in-one computers also are available in screen sizes that can view two full-sized pages of paper music at once.

Hybrid Options

But what if you are greedy and want the best of both worlds – the mobility of a smaller computer combined with the larger screen-viewing options of a desktop computer?

One option is to forego the desktop computer itself (the box "brain") and just get a monitor (or even a digital TV!) that can accommodate a direct cable connection to your mobile computer of choice. You will need to *make sure* that your monitor or TV has the necessary ports to accept your computer's output, and that your computer or tablet has the capability to connect to an external monitor. There are a whopping array of options, ranging from the granddaddy VGA connector to S-video, and the more modern HDMI, and now the new Thunderbolt I/O from Apple.

Another option is to use both a desktop or all-in-one computer AND a mobile computer. You can use software to project the screen of your mobile computer onto the monitor of the larger stationary computer. In most cases, you will need a Wi-Fi (wireless Internet) connection to make this work, but it's a great way to teach and work in an ensemble setting, for example. One great example of this kind of software is Reflector for the iPad (http://www.reflectorapp.com/), which works with both Mac and PC computers.

Projecting my iPad screen wirelessly to my HP Touchsmart All-In-One computer, using Reflector

Conductors routinely pooh-pooh tablets for being way too small for viewing their massive oversized scores, which can typically measure at least 13-17 inches in height for full symphonic works. Desktop computers large enough to accommodate those sizes – even hybrid ones – are an impractical solution for lugging on and off stage and through crowded airport terminals. But we're finally starting to see a new wave of super-sized tablets that are dipping an experimental toe in the proverbial market waters that might be large enough – and relatively portable enough – to assuage the ire of even the most Toscanini-tempered stick swinger.

Here's an eye-popping new 27-inch hybrid tablet from Lenovo that runs a full version of Windows 8, with a hinge that makes it easy to prop either as a desktop or fold back as a bona-fide tablet.

The 27-inch Lenovo Horizon Tablet

Screen Aspect Ratios

One final consideration in your search for the ultimate sheet music-reading computer will be to consider a geeky number called the screen's aspect ratio. An aspect ratio is a set of numbers describing the width relative to the height of a rectangular shape. Why is this important? It really only becomes an issue if you're used to seeing paper as – well, "paper." A typical 8.5"x11" piece of paper has an aspect ratio of roughly 4:3. On an iPad, that works out pretty well, and you'll see a sheet of scanned sheet-music paper looking like it properly fits within the screen:

An 8.5"x11" piece of sheet music displayed on an iPad with a 4:3 screen aspect ratio

But if you're considering a computer with a different aspect ratio – say, 16:10, which is the most common screen aspect ratio for Android and Microsoft 8 computers/Surface tablets these days – you'll end up with that piece of paper not quite filling out the entire screen space, despite the touted size of the screen.

Oops...can you say, "hanging chad"?

If you're working with text files and an app that can dynamically resize the fonts, this won't be an issue since you're working with a dynamic file format as opposed to a static snapshot of a paper page, and the text will fill the page regardless of the aspect ratio. More on dynamic vs. static sheet music in chapter 25.

CHAPTER NINETEEN

Finding the Perfect Digital Sheet-Music Reader, Part 1: Giants

Consider the lowly bean.

Beans are beneficial, but – let's face it – they're basically boring. Bland taste and pasty texture, right? But wait! What if you discovered that they actually were magical beans, Jack? A whole new reality, right?

Working with digital sheet music is a bit like dealing with beans. You can settle for a computer that functions as a high-tech music binder, or you can find the right combination of applications and computer to open an incredible new world of possibilities. Which brings us to the third question you need to answer: *What do you want to see?*

Well, Jack, there are three ways you can go – fe, fi, fo ... oh, never mind ...– but your software and hardware combos will give you these choices: **Giants**, **Rainbows**, or **Crystal Balls**.

Giants (or how much does size matter ... to you?)

With digital sheet music, an enlarged view is limited only by the size of your screen and the reader application. Depending on whether you work with static sheet-music files such as PDFs, or dynamic ones such as text files, you'll have different options for resizing your music.

In the case of static files, several applications offer the option to view PDF files a half page at a time. On a tablet, rotating the tablet to its side typically does this. On a desktop or laptop computer, this would be a selectable option within the program. For both tablets and computers, this half-page view takes advantage of the screen's width ratio to effectively zoom the page – the larger the screen, the bigger the zoom. In the case of an iPad or Android tablet, a half-page view makes the music the same size as paper versions. And with a desktop computer or a laptop connected to an external display, your zoom level is limited only by the size of your monitor screen. Imagine connecting your computer to one of those new fangled, impossibly thin 80-inch LCD television sets and reading your music that way. Throw away the bifocals, Magoo!

A full-page view of music on the iPad using forScore

A half-page, zoomed view of the same music on the iPad

With dynamic sheet music such as text files, you don't have to worry about viewing by page increments. You can adjust viewing factors, such as font size and type, and sometimes line spacing, depending on the application. With this level of dynamic zoom control, it's conceivable that you could read your text on much smaller devices like an iPhone or an iPod Touch, and completely forego the bulk of a larger device.

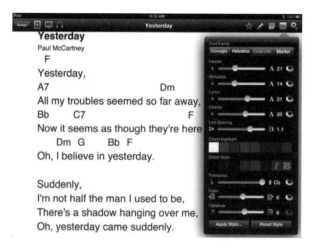

Font options using OnSong on the iPad

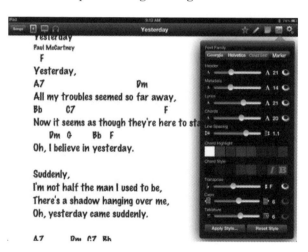

Changing font type with OnSong on the iPad

Yet another font style

Now, let's take a look at **Rainbow** capabilities, you colorful person, you.

CHAPTER TWENTY

Finding the Perfect Digital Sheet-Music Reader, Part 2: Rainbows

Color my world, you say?

Well, several applications give you practically unlimited ability to annotate and mark up static PDF files with digital ink and highlights. You can scribble on your digital sheet music to your heart's content, in a wild display of colors, and just as easily erase it all without damaging the music. Try doing that with color pens and highlighters on your paper sheet music!

Annotated PDF sheet music on an iPad running the forScore app

Applications that work with dynamic files typically don't have the capability to add digital-ink annotations, but you can still apply colors in creative ways. In this example, using an iPad app called OnSong, you can highlight the chord symbols in one color, then change the chord font color so that it's different from the lyric font color, giving you a clearer distinction between what is played and what is sung.

Using color in OnSong to highlight chord symbols in text files

CHAPTER TWENTY-ONE

Finding the Perfect Digital Sheet-Music Reader, Part 3: Crystal Balls

Yes, you *can* see into the future.

If you read music that takes up enough pages to require a page turn, then you've experienced what I call the "blind zone." When you get to the last note of the last measure of the last page, you cannot see what's coming up next – you are in the "blind zone," and if you're in a performance situation you have only a split second to turn the page to see what's next. Classical pianists actually hire people to sit next to them to take care of the pesky page-turning task, but I'm sure every one of them could recount some horror story where the page was turned too soon or too late, ruining the flow of the performance (You may recall my tragic page-turning tale in chapter 1).

Several applications have a nifty feature by which you can eliminate the blind zone entirely and always see what's coming next in the music. If you're viewing your music on a monitor large enough to display two pages at a time, you can set up the page turns so that you only change one page at a time. Here's how it works:

- You start by seeing page 1 on the left and page 2 on the right.
- When you "turn" the page, you now see page 3 on the left and page 2 on the right.
- "Turn" the page again, and now you see page 3 on the left and page 4 on the right.

Viewing two pages of sheet music in MusicReader PDF 4

With a half-page turn, you see page 2 on the right and the next page 3 on the left for a continuous view

The next page turn completes the view from page 3 to page 4

It sounds a bit confusing at first, but trust me – if you can get your head around the idea that you don't need to turn two full pages at a time, and can actually have a continuous unobstructed view of your music, you'll realize what a revolutionary idea this is. No more blind zones, and you can always see what's coming up next!

If you're working off of a single-page view, there are applications that can apply a similar "look ahead" capability. Here's how it works:

1. You see a full page of music (page 1).
2. When you "turn" the page, the page splits, showing you the present page on the bottom half (page 1) and the next page on the top half (page 2).
3. "Turn" the page again, and now the split disappears, showing the next full page of music (page 2).

A full-page view of music using forScore on an iPad

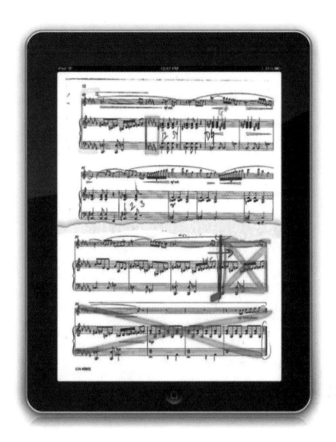

Turning half of the page in forScore

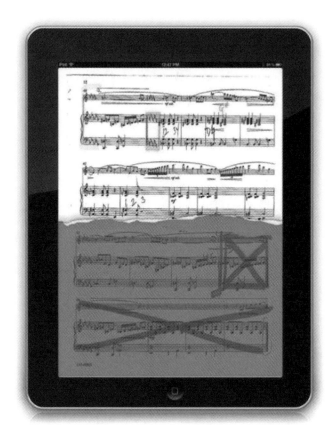

Note the previous page can be seen on the bottom half ...

... and the next page can be seen on the top half

Of course, being able to continuously look ahead means turning the digital page more frequently. That may sound like a drawback, but I'll explore how even page turns can be effortless when we get to the chapter on "Controllers" (chapter 35 for all you look-ahead readers).

The above examples primarily apply for static PDF sheet-music files. For dynamic text files, you can find applications for scrolling the view in a manner similar to a teleprompter, the device that presidents and newscasters use to be able to read speeches and scripts in a continuous manner.

When I started my paperless journey 12 years ago, there were only one or two applications that gave me the ability to view and mark up my music with digital ink. It's been amazing to watch the explosion of music-reading applications in recent years, giving me options I couldn't even dream of needing but now realize that I can't live without. Throughout it all, my core library has continued to grow and port itself from machine to machine. With each new device, it's been astonishing to experience the incredible rate at which technology improves. As you narrow your search down for the perfect digital sheet-music-reading computer, keep in mind that in some ways it will be a never-ending search, but the reward is in the journey as you discover the amazing possibilities that make it impossible to go back to paper.

To summarize:

1. Start with the application before deciding on a device
2. Determine if your needs are for a mobile, stationary, or a hybrid device
3. Realize that you may discover a completely new way to look at your music

You will find a great resource for comparing sheet-music applications on various tablets and computers at http://airturn.com/appguide

CHAPTER TWENTY-TWO

Content, Part 1: An Overview of Digital Sheet-Music Sources

The second "C" in the digital sheet-music setup is Content, i.e. the files that will make up your sheet-music library. There are three primary sources for sheet music content:
1. Paper
2. Internet
3. Composition

Paper

We already covered the steps involved in converting your paper sheet-music library to digital PDF files in Chapter 5, "The 5th C: The Art of Converting Paper to PDFs". Aside from the "Jeeves" option of getting a book scanning service to scan your music collection for you, I meet many musicians who balk at the time and energy it would take to scan their entire library – kind of like converting all their cassettes and vinyl to CDs, right? The enormity of the task stops them cold in their tracks, making the prospect of becoming a digital musician about as appealing as peeling a warehouse full of potatoes.

When I started the transition towards becoming a paperless pianist, my paper-music library was housed in two enormous wall shelves outside my office at Curtis. They were stacked floor to ceiling with alphabetized filing boxes. My library was so large, I needed a rolling stepladder to get to the boxes on the top shelves! But rather than getting discouraged at the size of my digital Everest, I just focused on scanning the three or four pieces I needed for the next few days.

It's amazing how quickly your digital library will grow with just 15 minutes of scanning a day. As the proverbial saying goes, the way to eat an elephant is one small bite at a time (my vegan friends cringe at the thought, but you get the idea ...).

Another helpful perspective is to consider how much time you spend organizing, searching for, and then re-filing your paper music collection (and if you are as absent-minded as I am, add in the time you spend re-tracing your steps to find that piece of music you left in a practice studio or in a backstage dressing room). If you apply the time you would normally spend searching for your physical sheet music into scanning, you'll find that – at least in the beginning – the time spent working with your music nets pretty evenly. As your library grows, you'll find yourself scanning less and less frequently. Before you know it, you'll be enjoying the benefit of having everything that you need with you at all times, and it will be instantaneously searchable.

No more messy stacks of books and binders. No more time wasted searching for that piece of music buried in your collection. No more headaches over re-filing your collection (or dealing with the aftereffects of procrastinating that task). And best of all, no more stress over forgetting to bring that part, or discovering that your music is on its way, without you, to some nice Croatian beach resort because the airline misrouted your luggage.

Internet

On April 12, 2009, _The New York Times_ reported on the closing of a small sheet-music store a stone's throw away from Carnegie Hall. For more than six decades, Patelson's had been a musical Mecca for classical musicians. They browsed through its musty stacks of sheet-music bins and worked up the courage to ask an indignant employee about the best edition for Chopin Etudes or the availability of an obscure work by Szymanowski.

Patelson's passing highlighted the new realities of the digital age for retail sheet music. And with the powerful advent of tablet computers such as the iPad, we're on the brink of seeing another transformation – from online shopping and physical delivery of paper sheet music (a la Amazon Books) to downloading digital versions directly into tablets and computers (a la Amazon Kindle).

In "Content, Parts 3-8," we'll take a look at both a wide range of websites providing digital sheet music – free and commercial – as well as the types of sheet-music files that these sites provide, what you can do with these files, and some recommended apps to make the most of them.

Composition

Before you scrawl another line of lyrics on that cocktail napkin or pen another phrase to that symphony, you'll want to think about a single word that could forever change the way you think about composing your own music:

Martians.

Yep, Martians. Trust me, it has everything to do with shifting the way you think about creating music – not just with the "how" (using digital tools, naturally), but more importantly, "why," hopefully resulting in, "whoah!" The "what" will deal with the type of music you create, whether it's written with words or crafted with traditional music notation. And the "where"? Trust me, in the digital realm, "where" always means, "everywhere," which is exactly where you want your music to be, right?

If I have you scratching your head over this supposed "overview" of composition as a source for digital sheet music and you have the attention span of an ADD artist missing their Ritalin prescription, jump to chapter 31 titled, "So You Wanna Be a Beatle?"

CHAPTER TWENTY-THREE

Content, Part 2: Apps for Reading Paper Sheet-Music Sources

As we discussed in Chapter 5, paper sheet-music needs to be converted to PDF files by using a scanner (or a scanning app from your smartphone – or Jeeves). In essence, you are really just taking digital pictures of each page.

Once you have your PDF files assembled, the next step is to decide which app or program you want to use to read – and perhaps mark up – your digitized music. In general, "app" is the term used for mobile devices such as tablets and smartphones; "program" is the term used for more traditional computers running Microsoft Windows and Apple OS X operating systems. Keep in mind that while your reader app/program options will be determined by the operating system running on your reading device du jour, your PDF files themselves are universal in nature, so it's pretty easy to migrate them between devices. But ...

Got Ink? Beware!

One caveat: if marking up your music with annotations is a high priority, you'll want to be aware of the limitations on portability of those markings. While the source PDF itself is a universal file, the added layer for digital-ink annotations is not, and every app/program developer comes up with different ways to work with that ink layer. In other words, the markings you make in one app/program generally aren't viewable in any other app/program. Fortunately, some apps/programs give you the option to "bake in" the ink layer. The ink markings you make become a permanent part of the source PDF, meaning you won't be able to change or erase them, kind of like the sailor's "I Love Rosie" tattoo he got while on shore leave. Keep that in mind if you need to juggle between "clean copies" and ones that are inked up.

PDF Apps/Programs

Given that the PDF is a universal file format, there are literally hundreds if not thousands of apps and programs for reading these types of files. To help narrow down the field, I'll point out PDF readers that either are specifically designed with musicians in mind, or at least offer sheet-music-friendly features worth considering. I'll list a number of basic factors:

- the ability to add annotations
- the ability to export those annotations to other PDF readers
- the ability to create set lists (set lists give you the ability to select a number of songs, put them in any order, and have the app/program automatically open each song in succession as if they were put together into one big binder)
- one cool feature that's worth considering

By the way, all the apps/programs below are compatible with external page-turning devices like the **AirTurn** – after all, what's the point of reading music digitally if you can't enjoy a bit of digital moxie and be able to turn pages hands free?

Here is a list of PDF sheet-music-reader apps and programs, broken down by device and/or operating system:

iPad

At the time of this writing, notwithstanding the surge in popularity of a plethora of Android tablets made by a tizzy of manufacturers, the iPad is still the undisputed champion of the tablet world. With its commanding market share and relatively uniform design across four generations (and one shrink-ray mini-me version), the iPad has attracted the broadest pool of developers writing apps for reading PDF sheet-music files. Here's an alphabetical listing of PDF-reading apps for the iPad (all generations):

Calypso Jam

- Annotations: No
- Annotation export: No
- Set Lists: Yes
- Cool Feature: Supports 25 fake books. That means that if you happen to have a PDF version of a supported fake book, each song is automatically indexed for super-fast searches and some innovative page-layout options to maximize the view of your music on the diminutive iPad screen.

Chromatik

- Annotations: Yes
- Annotation export: Sort of (see below)
- Set Lists: Yes
- Cool Feature: All your sheet music – both PDF files and sheet music purchased from the Chromatik store – is synced over the web. That means you can share you music with your band mates and students, and they can view all the latest annotations you make as well.

DeepDish GigBook

- Annotations: Yes
- Annotation export: No
- Set Lists: Yes
- Cool Feature: If you have a large PDF file containing dozens or hundreds of songs, you can create - "super bookmarks" to extract the songs you want to use so that you don't have to keep flipping pages to go from one song to the next.

forScore

- Annotations: Yes
- Annotation export: Yes
- Set Lists: Yes
- Cool Feature: You can create multiple versions of a song. This is great for collaborative pianists who have to accompany 14 versions of the Tchaikovsky Violin Concerto and want to be able to have customized marked-up copies for each rendition.

iGigBook

- Annotations: Yes, sort of (more like typed Post-It notes)
- Annotations export: Yes, sort of (can be shared with other iGigBook users)
- Set Lists: Yes
- Cool Feature: A fake book lover's dream app, iGigBook has done the hard work of indexing more that 60 popular jazz fake and real books, making searches for any song (as well as searches by composer and key) within those collections a breeze.

Music Binder

- Annotations: No
- Annotation export: No
- Set Lists: Yes
- Cool Feature: Got a big collection of songs? Need to pull up a song in a jiffy? Music Binder features the fastest – and I really mean, the fastest – system for instantly finding any song in your collection, thanks to an innovative on-screen keyboard system. The developer claims you can find any song in one second. Guess what? He's right!

MusicPodium for iPad

- Annotations: Yes
- Annotation export: No
- Set Lists: No
- Cool Feature: Your music is listed as picture snippets of the front page, in addition to the title and composer, making it easy to see the first few measures of the piece at a glance.

MusicReader PDF for iPad

- Annotations: Yes
- Annotation export: No
- Set Lists: Yes
- Cool Feature: You can annotate your music pretty quickly while turning pages hands free with a page-turning pedal such as the AirTurn. It's nice not to have to tap extra buttons to open and close the annotating feature each and every time you need to draw some ink on the page.

My Lyric Book

- Annotations: No
- Annotation export: No

- Set Lists: Yes
- Cool Feature: My Lyric Book automatically networks across multiple iPads. That means that as long as everyone has My Lyric Book installed and the same collection of sheet music files, anyone can select a song and everyone else's iPad will automatically open to that same song. Talk about staying on the same page!

NextPage for iPad

- Annotations: Yes
- Annotation export: No
- Set Lists: Yes
- Cool Feature: Nice user interface, including a numbered navigation page bar that makes it easy to quickly jump to any part of the piece.

OnSong

- Annotations: No (you can add "sticky notes," but not ink annotations)
- Annotation export: No
- Set Lists: Yes
- Cool Feature: OnSong is optimized for text files (we'll revisit OnSong in a later chapter), but it works well as a PDF scroller – instead of viewing page turns one full page at a time, you can set OnSong to vertically scroll a customizable amount of the page at variable speeds. Very handy when you need to look ahead beyond page breaks.

piaScore HD

- Annotations: Yes
- Annotation export: No
- Set Lists: No
- Cool Feature: If your iPad has a front facing

camera, you can turn pages by turning your face away from the screen. Might not be the best feature if you wildly gesticulate at the piano like Lang Lang, but you can always turn this feature off and use an AirTurn page turning pedal instead.

Planning Center Music Stand

- Annotations: Yes
- Annotation export: No
- Set Lists: Yes ... sort of (set lists aren't created within the app itself; rather, they're created and shared with team members via the www.planningcenteronline.com web service)
- Cool Feature: This app is a companion for the Planning Center Online web service, and is optimized for worship teams that need to share schedules, sheet-music PDFs, and playlists. No more excuses like "the dog ate my hymnal"!

Scorecerer

- Annotations: Yes
- Annotation export: No
- Set Lists: Yes
- Cool Feature: Wirelessly sync files between your iPad and your computer.

Set List Maker

- Annotations: No
- Annotation export: No
- Set Lists: Yes (duh – see the name of the app!)
- Cool Feature: Primarily intended for audio file playlist control, you can link PDF files to songs as lyric sheets. Best used for text reading.

TheGigEasy app for iPad

- Annotations: Yes
- Annotation export: No
- Set Lists: Yes
- Cool Feature: Nice-looking controls that can be moved anywhere on the page and tucked away for unobstructed views of your music.

Tonara

- Annotations: Sort of (limited to music notation stamps)
- Annotation export: No
- Set Lists: No
- Cool Feature: Any song purchased from the Tonara store can take advantage of the app's signature feature, the ability to listen to you play and turn pages accordingly. If you import PDF files, you can turn pages with an AirTurn pedal instead. Note that the automatic "listen & turn" feature only works with Tonara-specific files. Currently there is a limited store selection (what? no "Star Wars Theme" by John Williams?) but hopefully that will grow in the future.

unrealBook

- Annotations: Yes
- Annotation export: No
- Set Lists: Yes
- Cool Feature: Link multiple iPads to do everything from opening everyone's songs to turning everyone's pages from a master iPad. Talk about keeping everyone on the same page!

Mac/PC

The text-centric form factor of the laptop computer prevents it from mass adoption by musicians as a digital sheet-music reader. Tablet PCs made a valiant effort for more than a decade, but they tend to be priced too high for most musicians' wallets. Nevertheless, here are some viable options for Mac and PC computers, particularly if you are looking for a viewing screen that doesn't force you to squint or reconsider Lasik eye surgery.

PDF Annotator

- Annotations: Yes
- Annotation export: Yes
- Set Lists: No
- Cool Feature: PDF Annotator was never designed specifically for musicians, but it features the smoothest, most natural inking experience of any program on any device. Ideal for heavy annotators. Best experienced using a digital pen on a tablet PC computer.

MusicReader PDF 4

- Annotations: Yes
- Annotation export: Yes
- Set Lists: Yes
- Cool Feature: Multiple page-view options, including customizable half-page views to optimize the fit and zoom of a vertical page on a horizontal screen, and two-page views for computer screens/monitors large enough to display two full pages of music at a time.

Android

The strange paradox is that while there are tons of Android tablets in all shapes and sizes, there still is a paucity of PDF-reading apps adequate for musicians. Developers complain that there is little to no money to be made making Android apps, so that may be the main reason we don't have many options yet. But with Android tablets now outselling iPads, you can be sure that we'll start to see many more PDF reading apps for musicians in the near future.

Cool Reader
- Annotations: No
- Annotation Export: No
- Set Lists: No
- Cool Feature: This app is designed primarily as an eBook reader, so now you can sneak in a chapter or two from the latest Michael Connelly detective thriller while waiting for your next Brahms symphony tuba solo.

EbookDroid
- Annotations: No
- Annotation export: No
- Set Lists: No
- Cool Feature: If you don't like the glow of a tablet screen in a dark performance setting, you can reverse the colors of the sheet music, making the page black and the notes white. Takes a little getting used to, but very effective for cutting down on making your face look like an apparition.

ezPDF Reader PDF Annotator

- Annotations: Yes
- Annotation Export: Yes
- Set Lists: No
- Cool Feature: Annotations!   Draw and mark up your PDF files to your heart's content.   You can even play non-Flash multimedia files embedded into the file in case you just have to watch that Looney Tunes cartoon while playing that Carl Stalling score...

MobileSheets for Android

- Annotations: Yes
- Annotation export: No
- Set Lists: Yes
- Cool Feature: Besides the fact that as of this writing it is pretty much the ONLY PDF reader specifically for musicians in the Android market? Keep your eye on this app, as lots of features are constantly being added. It's only a matter of time before it will be able to hold its own compared to other PDF readers regardless of device or operating system.

Polaris Office 4.0

- Annotations: No
- Annotation Export: No
- Set Lists: No
- Cool Feature: This isn't an app specifically for musicians per se, but you can read virtually any document format with it, including PDFs, text and Word documents natively.

I've only scratched the surface of most of these apps' capabilities. If you'd like to search for apps by what they can do, you can go to AirTurn's App Guide, which works like an expanding outline tree. Here's the URL: http://airturn.com/appguide

Now let's take a slight detour and take quick look at putting your music together into set lists.

CHAPTER TWENTY-FOUR

Content, Part 3: Set Lists

If you play music in a worship setting, or perform a recital with more than one work on the program, or shuttle between wedding gigs and nightclub sets, you know what it means to work with a set list. In the paper world, a set list can look like a formal printed program listing the order of pieces to be performed for both the audience and the performer's benefit:

The Curtis Institute of Music
Roberto Díaz, President

2008–09 Student Recital Series
The Edith L. and Robert Prostkoff Memorial Concert Series

◆

Ninety-Seventh Student Recital
Graduation Recital—Brittany Sklar, violin, with Hugh Sung, piano
Thursday, May 14 at 5:15 p.m.
Field Concert Hall

◆

Adagio in E major, K. 261	Wolfgang Amadeus Mozart
Rondo in C major, K. 373	(1756–91)
Sonata No. 2 in A major, Op. 100	Johannes Brahms
Allegro amabile	(1833–97)
Andante tranquillo—Vivace	
Allegretto grazioso (quasi andante)	
Preludes for Piano	George Gershwin
transcribed by Jascha Heifetz	(1898–1937)
Allegro ben ritmato e deciso	
Andante con moto e poco rubato	
Allegro ben ritmato e deciso	

Brittany Sklar, violin
Hugh Sung, piano

Or it can look like a hand-scrawled magic marker shopping list for the band's eyes only:

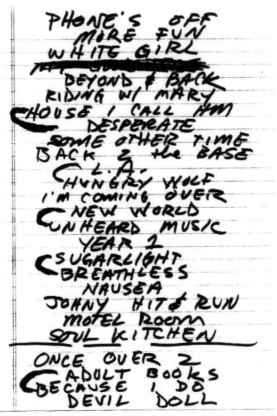

Obviously, the longer the program, the more books and binders that need to be shuffled on stage, creating the real potential for an awkward paper-flipping ruckus between pieces. Thankfully, the digital sheet-music revolution does away with this archaic bit of musical Rolodex-ing with apps that have set-list capabilities (see the previous chapter).

While each app will have different methods for creating set lists, their features are pretty universal:

- Select songs from your digital sheet-music library
- Arrange them in any order
- Move or delete songs within the set list
- Name and save your set list
- Open songs automatically in the set-list order

Once your set list is created, you can either start from the beginning and read through all the pages of your music as if they were bound in a single big book, or jump to any specific song manually and continue in the set-list order from that song onwards.

Let's take a look at one example of creating a set list with an iPad app called TheGigEasy.

When you open TheGigEasy, you will see a menu bar on the bottom of the screen. Tap on the icon labeled "Set Lists," then tap on the "Add" button in the pop up window that appears if you want to create a new set list.

A new popup window will appear on the left side. This window will show a list of all the songs in your library. Tap on the songs you want to add to the set list in any order and they will appear on the set list window on the right.

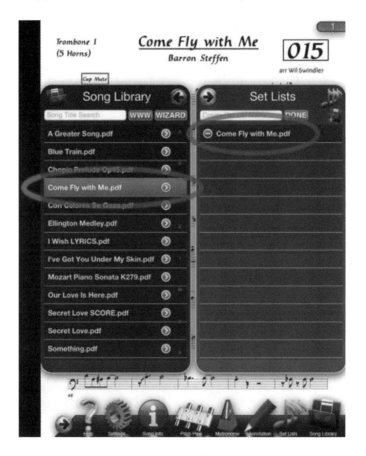

You can change the order of any song in your set list by tapping and holding the icon that looks like three bars next to each song listing. The panel containing the song will "pop out" and you'll be able to drag it to any position in your set list.

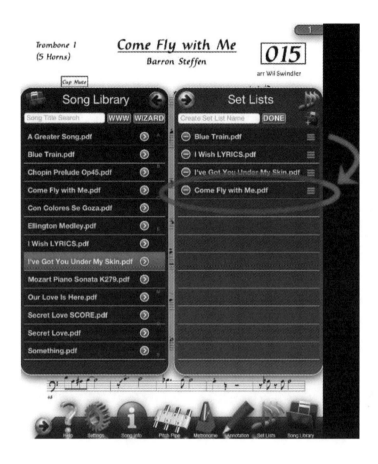

If you change your mind about a song and want to delete it from your set list, tap on the red circle with the white line in the middle next to the song. The circle will rotate and a "delete" button will appear to the right of the song. Tap on the "delete" button and POOF – your song is removed from your set list.

Don't forget to give your set list a memorable name in the white text box above, and tap "done" when you're done.

And with that, let the drum roll begin!

You can watch a video demonstration of creating a set list using TheGigEasy iPad app by going to this link:

http://www.airturn.com/grammy-musicians/solutions/grammy-awards/set-lists

Or by using your smartphone and scanning in this QR code:

Bwahahahahaha! Or, The Evil Megalomaniacal Set-List Master of the Universe

Hey, boys and girls! Now that you know how to make set lists, how would you like to really mess with your bandmates' heads? Some apps give you the evil ability to control multiple iPads from a master iPad and use your set lists so that you open everyone else's iPad to the same song automatically – and in some cases, even turn their pages for them! Bwahahahahahaha! Generally speaking, everyone will need a copy of both the app used as well as the digital sheet-music files being used. Here's a short list of apps that give you this evil power to forever banish the infernal question, "what are we playing next?"

My Lyric Book – this is actually a much more democratically inclined app. No "master/slave" relationships when using this one – *anyone* can open a song and everyone else's iPads will open to the same song. Infernal democracy indeed! At least no one can control anyone else's page turns with this app ... at least, not yet ... http://www.dctsystems.co.uk/Software/My_Lyric_Book/Welcome.html

OnSong – The master can send set list files to every slave iPad that's connected via OnSong's "OnCue" feature. The master can open everyone's songs. The master can scroll everyone's pages. All bow to the OnSong master! http://onsongapp.com/

Set Lists –This app only uses text files, but instead of turning pages, the app will cut up the song into phrases wherever there is a line break. The result? Faster opening of songs and near real-time phrase changes synced across all connected iPads. http://www.setlistsapp.com/

unrealBook – In addition to being able to exert master/slave control over multiple iPads reading PDF files, unrealBook can also be set to control a second iPad to always show the next page, mimicking the action of reading a full-sized book two pages at a time. Each page turn will advance only one page at a time, so you'll see page 1 on the left iPad with page 2 on the right iPad, then page 2 on the left iPad and page 3 on the right iPad, etc. http://www.diystompboxes.com/unrealbook/

As we've mentioned in previous chapters, you can explore many more apps by their evil-powered feature sets using AirTurn's interactive App Guide at http://airturn.com/appguide

Now, let's get back to our exploration of digital sheet-music content, leaving the terrestrial bounds of paper-based scores and launching warp speed towards a galaxy of Internet-based sheet music resources.

CHAPTER TWENTY-FIVE

Content, Part 4: An Overview of Internet Sheet-Music Sources

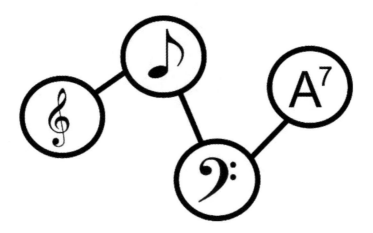

More and more, the question of "How do I get sheet music into my digital reader?" will be answered by downloadable options from the Internet. Presently, getting digital sheet music from the Internet is, in many respects, still a foray into the electronic "Wild, Wild West." There you'll find viable commercial options, as well as a staggering array of free ones from resources ranging from legitimate to dubious. Before I begin to list sites and apps, though, it might be helpful to get a bird's-eye view of some general aspects of the types of downloadable sheet-music files you'll find.

Static vs. Dynamic

PDFs created from scans of paper music are basically *static files* – in other words, you can read the music as it appears on the page, but you can't modify the notes other than to draw digital-ink markings or type text annotations on the page. For all intents and purposes, PDF files display music just like physical paper. You can't transpose the music into a different key or change the size of the printed notes other than by changing the zoom options or using a larger monitor.

Dynamic files, on the other hand, display music in formats that *can* be modified. Text files of lyrics can be edited to change the words, and font properties can be altered to modify its size, style and color. In some cases, chord symbols can be identified and transposed on the fly to any key. In the case of traditional music notation, not only can you transpose the music into any key, but (depending on the app) you can also hear the notes played back in a variety of tempi (speeds), and sometimes with different instrumentation for multi-part scores. Pretty slick, eh?

Portable vs. Proprietary

The universal nature of PDF and text files make them portable, that is, easy to migrate from computer to computer. This is great news for reading musicians, perhaps, but a commercial quandary for composers and publishers trying to make a living from selling sheet music. Thus, commercial sheet-music sources generally favor proprietary formats that either provide a limited number of times that you can physically print the music you purchase, or that can be read only in custom apps that can be used by licensed users, preventing them from copying and distributing their music beyond their own tablets and computers. Understandably, most free sites use portable file formats, while most commercial sites use proprietary files and custom readers. Let's take a look at resources for both types and discuss pros and cons for each.

CHAPTER TWENTY-SIX

Content, Part 5: Commercial PDF Sheet-Music Resources

Commercial PDF sheet-music sites are available for several genres of music. You can shop online, make your purchase, and then download the PDF files for use with your favorite PDF reader app or program. Here is some of what's available:

Classical Music

<u>Brassworks 4</u> – This is a niche classical site that's surprisingly comprehensive, offering PDF files for solo and ensemble brass configurations. Some of the offerings only are available as paper deliveries, but many are also available as PDF downloads. Founded by a retired brass ensemble made up of "three guys and a gal," this virtual sheet-music store came into existence out of fun and necessity when the group discovered that they had to write their own arrangements due to the dearth of available music for their configuration. http://brassworks4.com

<u>Every Note</u> – this is one of my favorite sites for commercial classical-music PDF files. You'll find a collection of more than 20,000 popular and hard-to-find scores representing more than 1,000 composers. The site was started by Soviet-born pianist Mark Zeltser, who made it his stated goal to offer "every classical note ever written." Dr. Zeltser maintains the site with the help of his programmer (who also happens to be his wife), Violetta. http://everynote.com

<u>Virtual Sheet Music</u> – this is a popular site for classical-music scores in PDF formats. It also offers jazz and popular tunes, but those files are in a proprietary Scorch format that limits you to printing paper versions rather than downloading portable PDF files. Virtual Sheet Music also provides a free iPad reader app for classical selections, and most offerings also include an MP3 audio file to help you hear how the music goes. Great for students and teachers. http://virtualsheetmusic.com

Educational

Mel Bay – Mel Bay provides an extensive library of educational PDF method eBooks and sheet-music collections. A fantastic resource for teachers and students of all instruments. http://melbay.com

Worship

PraiseCharts – PraiseCharts offers downloadable chord-chart and lead-sheet PDFs of popular Christian worship music, with transpositions in any key and orchestrated audio accompaniment tracks. http://praisecharts.com

SongSelect by CCLI – CCLI stands for Christian Copyright Licensing International, and is one of the major resources for purchasing licenses for the use of popular Christian music in worship settings. CCLI offers a paid membership service, called SongSelect, which gives you access to a vast library of worship music in a variety of downloadable formats, from lead sheets to chord and hymn sheets, to sound samples. http://us.songselect.com

CHAPTER TWENTY-SEVEN

Content, Part 6: Proprietary Sheet-Music Sites and Apps

Proprietary sheet-music sites represent a strange techno-schizophrenia when it comes to the future of music publishing. On the one hand, you have cutting-edge technology to sell and deliver commercial sheet music instantly over the Internet, eliminating the need to wait for physical shipping times or inventory availability at a brick & mortar store, while putting digital protections in place to prevent users from re-distributing copyrighted works en masse. Want the latest hit from Coldplay? Log in, pony up, and download. That's good.

On the other hand, these same digital tools keep sheet music shackled to Gutenberg-era handcuffs by forcing you physically print the music you buy. (Gutenberg, in case you forgot, is Johannes Gutenberg, the 15th-century inventor of the printing press.) Make sure you have paper in that printer, ink in that cartridge, and pray that nothing jams. That's silly.

Fortunately, with the powerful rise of tablet computers, we're beginning to see the emergence of a better option: proprietary sheet-music-reader apps. While still in developmental infancy, the marriage between Internet sheet-music content and proprietary reader apps is showing some promising signs of powerful digital progeny. Not only can you search, buy and download copyrighted content instantly, but also with some apps you can work more dynamically with your music than would ever be possible with printed-paper versions. Here's a sampling of what some of these reader apps enable you to do:

- Transpose instantly into any key
- Listen to audio playback of the notes at any tempo
- Add ink annotations to the music in multiple colors, and easily erase them
- Use one master ("conductor") device to open the same song on multiple ("slave") devices and, in some cases, turn everyone's pages and share ink annotation markings with everyone

Unfortunately, we have yet to see a universal reader app for all digital sheet music, so your purchasing decision may have just as much to do with what you want to be *able to do* with your music as with which *piece* you actually buy.

Here is a sampling of proprietary sheet-music sites and the apps that can be used to read them.

Musicnotes.com

As of this writing, musicnotes.com is the largest Internet site for commercial digital sheet music, with almost 250,000 works available for digital download. You can find arrangements of the latest hits, as well as popular tunes from yesterday for a wide variety of instruments.

App: Musicnotes Sheet Music Viewer
for iPad/Android

The companion app for the Musicnotes web store is a great example of what's possible when publishers grow beyond Gutenberg. If you've ever bought anything from Musicnotes.com in the past, once you log in with your username and password within the app, the entire archive of songs you've bought (and printed and lost) will auto-magically be available for download. The Musicnotes app enables users to draw ink and highlight markings on the music just like ink to paper. And its best feature? In the iPad version, you can set a "conductor" iPad to connect wirelessly to multiple "slave" iPads to open everyone's reader to the same song, turn everyone's pages, and even send text comments and ink markings to everyone (sorry, Android users are out of the loop with this megalomaniacal level of musical control over ensemble minions...)

Link to Musicnotes Sheet Music Viewer for iPad

Link to Musicnotes Sheet Music Viewer for Android

SheetMusicDirect.com

Don't let the numbers game fool you: even if SheetMusicDirect.com announced "only" 100,000 scores when it launched its reader app, the muscle behind the site and the app is none other than Hal Leonard, the world's largest sheet-music publisher. You'll find a tremendous depth of titles – from the latest hits and nostalgic goodies to jazz and classical compositions. It's encouraging when you see a publisher of this size and influence diving into the digital revolution – hopefully this will spur other publishers to follow suit ... sooner rather than later.

App: Sheet Music Direct for iPad

Sheet Music Direct for iPad is a more dynamic app in many ways. You can dynamically transpose the music into any key and listen to digital playback in any tempo. If there are multiple instruments in the score, you can alter or mute the playback volume individually for each track. You can even set up a click track and tap out your own tempo with the built-in metronome feature! One drawback is the lack of annotation features – the type of dynamic file the Sheet Music Direct's app uses (Sibelius Scorch) does not lend itself to adding an inking layer as do static PDF readers. Speaking of PDF files, Sheet Music Direct for iPad has the ability to import PDFs, so you could conceivably create a set list mixed with the latest top-10 hits, and the opus you wrote by hand on your napkin, and then scanned.

Link to Sheet Music Direct for iPad

CHAPTER TWENTY-EIGHT

Content, Part 7: Free Sheet-Music Sites – Classical Resources

Free? Did someone say, "free?" Yesiree, thar's gold up in them cyber clouds! Free for the taking – if you don't mind wading through buckets of shale to find yer treasure, that is. Old gold's the best, Sonny Boy – stuff that's been waylaid in musty warehouses and library catacombs suddenly find themselves pristinely preserved and free for the takin', thanks to the wonders of public domain and a faithful army of anonymously scurvy scanners scattered as far as the virtual eye can see.

Then, there's the digital underbelly, "full of scum and villainy." As Obi-Wan Kenobi might say, "We must be cautious," particularly when it comes to dubious copyright issues. But that doesn't seem to stop the explosion of sites that shower the virtual silicon streets with enough lyrics, chord charts and guitar tabs for the latest and greatest popular hits to make even the most moribund emo-lescent riff shredder smirk with glee.

Generally speaking, free sheet-music sites offer their wares in one of two file flavors: PDFs, the universal picture-book darling format; and text files, for musicians who like their music served up with consonants and vowels rather than black dots and race-track staff lines. To give you a comprehensive overview of the free sites available would be another Moby Dick tome in itself – I'll let Google be your guide down the branching rabbit holes. At the very least, here's a broad sampling of some of the best-known sites to satiate the most ravenous tablet/computer hard drives:

Classical/Public Domain

The International Music Score Library Project – IMSLP.org
File format: PDF

IMSLP, five sweet letters of the alphabet that sing to the classical musician's Wi-Fi antenna like few others, is the mother lode of all digital-sheet-music sites, the portal to an incredible repository of (at the time of this writing) nearly 60,000 works and 215,000 scores, representing almost 8,000 composers. And to think this incredible cyber-monument to the world's greatest musical compositions was begun by a bored 19-year-old conservatory student one winter month in 2006 (see *The New York Times* article "Free Trove of Music Scores on Web Hits Sensitive Copyright Note," by Daniel J. Wakin, Feb. 22, 2011). If you're looking for a piece of classical music in the public domain, there's an excellent chance that you'll find a version of it on IMSLP. Availability will vary depending on the copyright laws of each country (the site tries to flag works restricted by copyright accordingly – some works will be available in the U.S.A. but not the E.U., and vice versa). Gorge yourself accordingly.

Choral Public Domain Library – CPDL.org
File formats: PDF, Finale, Sibelius, among others

In an age where smartphones are obsolete minutes after they become available, having a site that's been around since 1998 is akin to being prehistoric. The brainchild of Rafael Ornes, CPDL is the largest online resource of choral music in the public domain, making available for free (at the time of this writing) more than 14,600 scores by more than 2,060 composers in a variety of file formats. If you like to sing with friends, this site is sure to make you get along even more harmoniously.

217

Sheet Music Consortium – http:// digital2.library.ucla.edu/sheetmusic/index.html
File format: PDF

This is like the music inter-library loan system on steroids. Sheet Music Consortium is an incredible collaboration between several major universities (Johns Hopkins U., Duke U., Indiana U., and the National Library of Australia, to name a few) and the Library of Congress to make their digital-sheet-music collections available for online viewing and study, and in many cases, even as PDF downloads. Of particular note are the vast collections of early American Songs, giving a vivid look into the evolution of popular music as a cultural phenomenon.

Scholarly Editions

Yes, it's true – the best things in life really *are* free! Here are some examples of online scholarly editions that no serious classical musician should overlook:

Wolfgang Amadeus Mozart: Neue Mozart-Ausgabe – http://dme.mozarteum.at/DME/nma/start.php?l=2
File format: Image (JPEG)

The Neue Mozart-Ausgabe is by far the best online resource for all of Mozart's works in a scholarly edition. The site states that usage is restricted to "personal study, educational and classroom use." The entire collection can be searched by category of work, a variety of KV catalogue numbers (KV, KV6, KV6 Anh. A B or C ... who in the world knew that so many librarians had so much time on their hands?), and even by key signature and preferred editor. Pages can be viewed a portion at a time by scrolling down the sidebar, or by clicking the page-number hyperlinks along the top. Beautiful typography makes viewing easy on the eyes and friendly for study. Kudos to the Internationale Stiftung Mozarteum and The Packard Humanities Institute for making this treasure of musical art freely available to the world!

The only drawback to this site is that the music is only available one page at a time. You can right-click and save each page individually (add a .jpg to the file name to have your computer recognize the image file in JPEG format), and then use a PDF converter to combine the images into a multi-page PDF file (I like iCombiner for Mac and doPDF for Windows).

Felix Mendelssohn: Digital Library Department of the Bavarian State Library - http://www.digital-collections.de/index.html?

c=autoren_index&l=en&ab=Rietz,%20Julius

File format: PDF

The Digital Library Department of the Bavarian State Library has an incredibly generous online offering for the classical-music community: the complete works of Felix Mendelssohn as digital scores, scanned in high quality for clear viewing. Scores are available as PDF downloads, but you need to navigate a bit of Bavarian German to assent to their download policies (I presume ... my German-reading skills are pathetic). This is an invaluable resource for serious musicians who can use these scores, readily available online, for the study and research of one of classical music's greatest musical masters.

For more wondrously free classical sheet-music links, visit http://airturn.com/sheet-music-sites/sheet-music-sites/free-sheet-music/classical-music

CHAPTER TWENTY-NINE

Content, Part 8: Free Text-Based Sheet-Music Sites

A little while back, I was working at a music trade show demonstrating how iPads could be used as digital sheet-music readers. Thinking like a classical musician, I assumed that setting up the iPads to display pages of – what else? – sheet music. Made perfect sense to me. This is what appeared on the iPad screens:

For the next couple of hours, I watched a steady stream of folks walk right past our booth. Every now and then someone would take a glazed glance over at our iPad farm, but then would continue on their way without so much as a skip in their step. I was perplexed. The iPad had just been introduced to the world with incredible fanfare – why didn't anyone share my geeky enthusiasm at how cool sheet music looked on the hottest piece of technology of the time? Then it hit me. Duh. I was thinking like a *classical* musician. I should've gotten a clue from the wail of electric guitars and thundering drum set riffs that filled the hall. I quickly changed the iPads to show *this*:

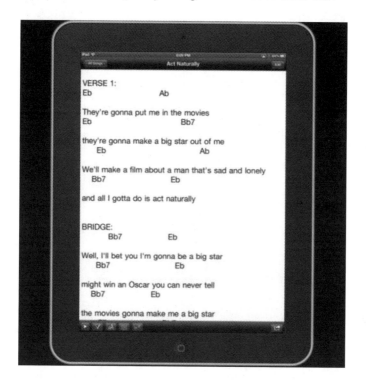

Almost immediately, a burly guy paused, pointed at one of the iPads, and remarked to his friend, "Hey, look! You can read *music* on this thing!" It just goes to show that one man's music is another man's hieroglyphics. To put this in perspective, *this* reads like hieroglyphics to me, but makes perfect sense to a jazz musician:

You say "to-*may*-to," I say "to-*mah*-to"... hey, no need to call the whole thing off, right? Whatever makes your digital sheet-music screen rock! As I hope my convoluted illustration explains, when I say "text-based sheet music," I'm referring to music primarily written using words and chord symbols, as opposed to calligraphic clefs, staff lines for "Every-Good-Boy-Doing-Fine," and black dots with flags, beams and racing stripes. Generally, there are four types of text-based sheet music:

- Lyrics only
- Lyrics and chords
- Chords only
- Tabs

As you can imagine, there are almost limitless online resources for text-based sheet music, the vast majority of which are free. More often than not, you'll start your Google search with the name of the song or the artist/band rather than worry about the file formats available, but it may still be helpful to see examples of sites that provide each of the four types of text-based sheet music so that you can narrow down what best suits your needs.

Lyrics only

If I were down to my last dollar -
Sittin' on an empty tank
I'd be a dollar richer than I was back-in-the-day
When I was playin' for tips and compliments
And half my rent was always spent on beer
Had a thousand dollar stereo
In a two hundred dollar truck
A screwdriver and some cussin'
Always made her start right up
But I tore it up one rainy night
Goin"round a curve when I hit second gear
And I'm just proud to be here

CHORUS

Lyrics from "Proud To Be Here," by Trace Adkins

Lyrics.com – How can you go wrong with a site name like that? You'll find lyrics to just about anything, especially popular songs of today, in languages spanning the globe. Many of the entries include embedded YouTube videos of the songs, so that you can hear how they go.

CowboyLyrics.com – Yippie-ky-yi-yay! Need I say more for lovers of country songs out there?
Lyrics and Chords

Chordie.com – This is another great resource for lyrics. You'll find some versions with chords included, but it can be hit or miss, so be prepared to click and wade.

WorshipArchive.com – This site has a nifty feature: You can transpose the chords (which appear in blue) to any key. You'll find contemporary worship songs, traditional hymn lyrics and chord progressions at this site.

Amazing Grace

Written by John Newton

| Ab | A | A# | Bb | B | C | C# | Db | **D** | D# | Eb | E | F | F# | Gb | G | G# |

```
VERSE 1:
D           D/F#        G           D
Amazing grace how sweet the sound
      D                  A
That saved a wretch like me
  D           D/F#       G       D
I once was lost, but now am found
      D         G   A  D
Was blind but now I see
```

Lyrics and chords for "Amazing Grace"

227

Chords Only

Chords-only example: "I got rhythm," by George Gershwin

JazzStudies.us – More than 1,200 jazz charts that can be transposed into any key on this site, then downloaded as image files (which can then be converted to PDF files and used in a PDF reader. See the section on PDF reader apps).

iReal b Forums – Based on the jazz-chord formats found in "The Real Book," this site actually is a discussion forum where users post collections of thousands of songs in a wide range of styles and genres. You'll only find chord progressions in these arrangements in the iReal b format – no lyrics, no melody lines written out, presumably in an attempt to prevent copyright issues. Keep in mind that you'll need to purchase install one of the iReal b applications for Mac, iOS or Android in order to be able to view and work with these files. We'll talk more about this in the upcoming text apps section. In the meantime, visit http://www.irealb.com/support for more information.

Tabs

```
We Are Never Ever Getting Back Together - Taylor swift

These are the chords that used in this song:
Caus  (330230)
Gaus  (330023)
D     (232000)
Emsus(330022)

Here's the tab. You can play it by repeating this through the entire song

E|---3-----------------------------2-----------------------------|
B|---3-------------3-3-------------3--------------0--0------------|
G|---------------0----0-----------------------0--------0---------|
D|---------2---2-------2-----------------2---2----------2--------|
A|---3----------3-----------------0--------2---------------------|
E|-------------------------------------------------------------- |

Thankyou for viewing my tab! Rate it please :D
```

Guitar Tab example: "We Are Never Ever Getting Back Together," by Taylor Swift

Tabs – short for "tablature," not "tabby cats" – are an innovative number/letter/hyphen system primarily for guitar players showing which frets to place your fingers on to strum chords (you can also find tabs for other instruments – see below). Basic tab sheets (on freebie sites) will show only the chords in succession within sections of a song; "pro" tab sheets (which you generally have to purchase) will include time signatures, measures, and rhythmic indications in the form of "note-less" stems and rhythmic flags/beams. On free sites, most of the non-pro tabs are arrangements of popular songs written by fans. Site visitors can vote for their favorite renditions, with the hope that the better versions climb to the top of the rankings.

Ultimate-Guitar.com – The tabs section of this mega-site does a great job of showing the type of arrangement along with the song title. You can find chords and "pro" tabs, along with the basic tab versions. The chord and tab versions are free, and you can sample some of the pro tab songs before making your purchase.

911Tabs.com – This site boasts access to more than three million tab arrangements of almost any song imaginable (within popular reason – no 12-tone Schoenberg arrangements here!) You'll find tabs for piano, bass and drums, as well as guitar. Transposable chord versions are also available for versions that include piano tabs.

Next, I'll take a look at applications that take advantage of the unique properties of text-based sheet music to be able to dynamically change things, such as the key of the song, the size of the words, and other features.

CHAPTER THIRTY

Content, Part 9: Text-Based Sheet-Music Apps

Text files are like Cinderella stories of the digital world. At first glance, their simplicity and utter lack of eye candy makes them look as worthless as a gumball ring in a Tiffany store.

Ah, but it's precisely their *lack* of excess code that makes them able to magically transform into the widest array of digital bling. Barebones text files are universally readable and readily adorned with enough malleable properties to make even Audrey Hepburn blush. (What's that you say? You never saw her in "Breakfast at Tiffany's?" Well then, how about Lady Gaga? Get the picture?) Resize your words! Slap on a vibrant coat of color! Dress it up with an eye-catching font! And with the right setup, even transpose your text chords into any key on the fly!

Whenever possible, you'll want to make sure your lyrics and chords are saved as text files (typically identified as file names with .txt at the end). That will ensure your previous words are given carte blanche to the widest availability of digital wardrobes. But even if your text-based music was created in Word (.doc files), Pages (.pages files) or Rich Text Format (.rtf files), you'll be able to find apps that can accommodate your digital flavor.

While you can work with word-processing programs to read your text files right off of a standard Mac or PC computer, you'll want to check out text reading apps specifically designed for today's digital sheet-music musicians. Here is a sampling of apps that work with iOS devices (iPad, iPhone, iPod Touch) and Android tablets, with a look at the text-file formats they can work with and a spotlight on one cool feature for each.

iOS Text Reader Apps

My Lyric Book – http://www.dctsystems.co.uk/Software/My_Lyric_Book

File Formats: Pages 09 (.pages), Word (.doc), PDF (.pdf), Rich Text Format (.rtf), Text (.txt)

Cool Feature: If everyone in your band is using iPads running My Lyric Book, you can have everyone sync together so that the band leader can open everyone's iPad to the same song. No more errant band members blaring the intro riff to the wrong song!

OnSong – http://www.onsongapp.com

File Formats: PDF (.pdf), Word (.doc), Pages (.pages), JPEG (.jpg), PNG (.png), TIFF (.tiff), ChordPro (.cho – we'll talk about this format in the next chapter), Text (.txt)

Cool Feature: OnSong is such a Swiss-Army-knife app that it's hard to pick just one cool feature, but a particularly handy one is OnSong's ability to search and pull down text lyrics right from within the app. It's built-in compatibility with Rockin' With The Cross (http://www.onsongapp.com/rwtc), an online Christian-worship-song resource, is a great example of synergy between app and content.

Set List Maker – http://www.arlomedia.com/apps/setlistmaker/main/home.html

File Formats: PDF, Word (.doc, .docx), PowerPoint (.ppt, .pptx), Pages (.pages), Keynote (.key), Rich Text Format (.rtf), Text (.txt), JPEG image (.jpg)

Cool Feature: Set List Maker is really all about its namesake: making and managing set lists. You can attach text documents containing your chord charts and lyrics to audio files and set the order of your songs for your shows accordingly. A musician's database dream come true.

Setlists – http://www.setlistsapp.com

File Format: Text (.txt)

Cool Feature: Setlists is designed to show your lyrics one phrase at a time. You can sync your iPads together in a band and not only open everyone's iPad to the same song, but also advance the lyrics a phrase at a time simultaneously. I've used this pun so many times it's wearing a groove in my keyboard, but here goes: This is a great way to – literally – keep everyone on the same page! (insert circus-seal laugh here)

SongBook Chordpro – http://linkesoft.com/ songbook/ios

File Formats: Chordpro (.pro, .chordpro, .chopro), Text (.txt), Tab (.tab, .crd)

Cool Feature: A true "gumball ring at Tiffany's" app. SongBook Chordpro's simple interface belies it's ability to manipulate text files in multiple ways, from transposing keys on the fly to changing font sizes and displaying fingering options for multiple instruments.

iReal b – http://www.irealb.com

File Format: Just like the cool kats of jazz, iReal b is an app that – while technically text based – really is in a league by itself, due to its proprietary file format. You can edit or create your own iReal b files either within the iReal b app, or by using the iReal b web editor at http://www.irealb.com/editor

Cool Feature: iReal b for iPad can play audio accompaniments to your tunes in any key. You can customize the output by adjusting the volume for (or muting) different instrument tracks, so that you can riff and shine like the star you are.

Android Text Reader Apps

Setlist Helper for Android -

http://www.setlisthelper.com/
File Format: Setlist Helper supports the Chordpro format
Cool Feature: Setlist Helper works in conjunction with http://setlisthelper.com, which is a web-based server for storing and keeping all your files in sync. Get accounts for all your band mates and you'll all have what you need in the right order streamed to all of your Android tablets lickity split.

Songbook –

http://linkesoft.com/songbook/android.html
File Format: Chordpro (.pro, .chordpro, .chopro), Text (.txt), Tab (.tab, .crd)
Cool Feature: Yup, you aren't seeing double here. Songbook is actually made by the same developer as SongBook Chordpro for iOS above. In fact, this clever developer makes versions of this nifty app for just about any computer platform (except for Linux...). Change font sizes, transpose into any key, and get fingering cheats for your favorite instrument.

The Fake Book -

https://play.google.com/store/apps/details?id=com.skrivarna.fakebook.android
File Format: Fakebook (proprietary file), text (iRealB/iRealBook/ABC notation format)
Cool Feature: Fakebook comes preloaded with chord progressions for more than a thousand of the classic jazz standards from The Real Book editions 1-5. Transpose your songs into any key. A jazz cat's dream come true!

Polaris Office 4.0 -

https://play.google.com/store/apps/details?id=com.infraware.polarisoffice4&hl=en

File Format: Text (.txt), Word (.doc), PDF

Cool Feature: This isn't an app specifically for musicians per se, but you can read virtually any document format with it, including PDFs, text and Word documents natively.

As we've mentioned in previous chapters, you can explore many more text reader apps by feature sets and operating systems using AirTurn's interactive App Guide at http://airturn.com/appguide

CHAPTER THIRTY-ONE

So You Wanna Be a Beatle?

Yeah, yeah, yeah?

You're sitting at your local Starbucks when a flash of inspiration has you reaching for a napkin, and before you know it you've scribbled your new platinum-selling song on crumpled pieces of soggy parchment, resorting to using your coffee stirrer to dab in the last precious lyrics. Or maybe you're having a Beethoven moment and you're using your driver's license as a straight edge to scratch out staff lines a measure at a time – all the while trying to ignore the perplexed gazes of barristers and other caffeine junkies.

If you're content to keep your masterpiece under bathroom lock and key, and croon your inspiration to your cat in the shower, then you can settle for the fact that your creation isn't lost to the compost bins of time. If, on the other hand, you actually want the rest of the world to revel in your song, you'll want to make your chicken scratch – you know – legible. And sharable. Beethoven might've had the benefit of uncontested genius to inspire legions of musicologists and editors to pore over his Jackson Pollock-inspired inkwell explosions to decipher his dots from his dashes, but the rest of us mere mortals might not have the benefit of academia to put up with hieroglyphics that are legible only to ourselves.

Beethoven's Cello Sonata Op. 69 ... I think

To that end, digital tools are an almost indispensable part of the modern musician's arsenal. If you're a Beatle or a Bob Dylan wanna-be, you don't need anything terribly fancy. In most cases just a text editor will suffice. But if you want to be another Beethoven or Bach, then you'll want to explore the wide range of digital-notation tools that turn your magnum opus into something that just begs to be read, played and published.

In the 20th century, just having a legible piece of music spit out of your inkjet printer might've been sufficient cause for narcissistic joy. But if I may expand your imagination for a minute, I'd like to take you on a quick trip to Mars.

When I was a kid in 1980, there was a cheesy TV mini series based on the 1950s Ray Bradbury sci-fi masterpiece, "The Martian Chronicles." In one of the opening scenes, a bald-headed Martian in flowing white robes sat contentedly in his home, running his fingers over a tablet while the narrator explained that he was listening to his book. *Listening* to his book! At the time, it sounded like such an alien concept. Of course, in today's age of Kindles and iPads we can stifle a little haute-tech chuckle, but the idea still bears strong consideration for today's musical scribes.

What if you could transfer your humble napkin scribbles into something that could actually sing back to you as you wrote them? Something that could be instantly transposable into any key, easily transmitted to all your band or orchestra members and, of course, heard with all the instruments playing on command all the musical ideas you heretofore only heard in your terrestrial-bound head?

Intrigued?

Today's technologies give you the ability to not only be your own publishing powerhouse, but also your own conductor, your own producer, to get instant feedback, and make changes on the fly.

In the next chapters, we'll show what to do if you want to be a Beatle or a Beethoven.

CHAPTER THIRTY-TWO

Cocktail Napkins, Canadians, and Chordpro

Once upon a time, in the far away land of Canada, two computer programmers by the names of Martin Leclerc and Mario Dorion came up with a magical way to turn hand-scrawled lyrics on cocktail napkins into beautiful, typeset lead sheets that were the fairest in the land (well, at least as fair as pimpled-paper dot matrix printers could grind out at the time). The year was 1991 – a magical year for Canadians, apparently, as the number-one song in all the world was sung by Canadian singer-songwriter Bryan Adams for the Kevin Costner movie "Robin Hood." Legend has it that Martin and Mario came up with the idea for a digital lead-sheet generating program while waiting 30 minutes for a tennis game, and the program "Chord" was born (and in a serendipitous note, Mario had his first date with his wife-to-be later that same day).

Appropriately, Bryan Adams' song "Heaven" was one of the sample songs included in the very first version of Chord. Canadian solidarity, eh?

Users of Chord started referring to the program as "ChordPro" for some unknown reason, and it was only a matter of time before websites began to appear offering lead sheets that took advantage of ChordPro's pretty-page-making capabilities (aka, "formatting" in geek-speak). ChordPro's popularity grew, but Martin and Mario faded into the mists of time and abandoned development of their program soon after their last 3.6.2 version in 1995.

In 2007, at the suggestion of a colleague named Adam Monsoon, Netherlands programmer Johan Vromans took up the Canadian programmers' mantle and produced Chordii (pronounced "chord-ee-ee," like a string-strumming chimpanzee, insists the developer – not "chordie," as frowned upon by www.chordie.com, which by the way is an excellent site). Johan managed to track down the original authors and convinced them to relicense the old program under GPL (GPL stands for General Public License, which means "free" in geek-speak). Chordii was then rebased on the liberated Chord sources. Being the programming guru that he is, Johan reworked the user guide, cleaned up the bugs, and got the program building and running again on modern computers, which by this time had the ability to see graphic fingering charts for approximately 360 guitar chords, as well as the capability for hapless guitarists to bravely contend with frog-throated singers who needed to change keys at the last minute.

Writing a song in ChordPro format is actually pretty simple. Trust me, you don't have to run in fear or cover your eyes at the sight of naked code – you basically type squiggly brackets around title and section elements (like "chorus" or "new song"), and square brackets around chord symbols. That's it, in a nutshell. Really.

Here's what ChordPro looks like under the coding hood, and the digital makeover results (source: h t t p : / / johan.vromans.org):

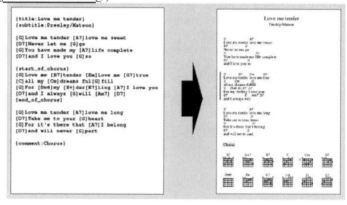

So why am I spending so much time recounting the history of an antiquated piece of software? Well, for one reason, it shows that people have been thinking about digital solutions to sheet music for a long time. More importantly, I'm hoping that you'll see how an itty bit of computer code can lead to a *lot* more flexibility when working with – and creating – your digital sheet music.

Before we plunge into the wide, wild world of online lyric- and chord-chart resources, let's get a global picture to better understand what's out there. To borrow a page from software developer John Grosberg, most online sheet music that's made up of lyrics and chords generally falls under three categories:

1. "Two-Line" style
2. "Rise-Up" style, based on " Rise Up Singing: The Group Singing Songbook"
3. ChordPro style

Two-Line style

A flash of musical inspiration hits during dinner – you reach for a napkin, scribble down some lyrics, and then work out a few chord symbols on top of the words. You've just created a "two-line" style lead sheet in its most basic form. If your band members can't decipher your chicken scratch, you use a text-writing program to make your coffee-stained masterpiece legible.

```
D                 C    D7   Em              A
Once she came in-to my room, feathered hat, and all,
```

(source: http://www.statistics101.net/chordsmith/)

Rise-Up style

The "Rise-Up" style tries to save space by putting all the chords for a verse in a single line. The slashes indicate which chords are used for each line in the verse – a relic of an era when music was printed on expensive pieces of mashed up wood pulp called "paper," with several sheets of this material sewn together in things called "books."

> A long, long time ago
> I can still remember how that music used to make me smile
> And I knew if I had my chance
> That I could make those people dance
> And maybe they'd be happy for a while
>
> / GD Em / Am7 C Em D / GD Em / Am7 C / Em Am D /

(source: http://www.guntheranderson.com/v/charts.htm)

For both the "Two-Line" and "Rise-Up" styles, there is a goofy word in computer speak: WYSIWYG. It's pronounced, "wizzy wig," and it's an acronym for the words, "What You See Is What You Get." Get it? Cute, eh? Geeky, for sure. Anywho, it pretty much means as it reads: what you see is what you get.

Translation: changes are a pain in the ... pen.

If you want to make the words bigger, you'll have to get a new napkin – er, make that a paper towel – and put on your best John Hancock penmanship. If your frog-throated singer wants to bring that song down from G to D, you'll have to manually go in and change each and every chord symbol accordingly or just rewrite the whole falutin' thing. So, in order to work with a format that empowers you to be simply and powerfully flexible, your choices are to either fire anyone who gets a cold or anyone who needs glasses.

This is where the "ChordPro" style comes in (cue drum roll and dramatic spotlight).

ChordPro style

The ChordPro style is the computer's attempt to replicate the "Two-Line" style by identifying which letters are chords and which words are – well, words. This distinction helps the computer to understand where to place the letter chords above the lyric words and, in many apps and programs, take advantage of that identification to be able to easily transpose those chord symbols to different keys, or change the look of the lyrics themselves (bigger, smaller, fancier, simpler, what have you). It's the "Two-Line" style with MacGyver smarts.

While ChordPro formats can't be used to turn a "Rise-Up" style into a "Two-Line" style, you can still transpose all the chords just as easily – they'll just have to stay cooped up in their slash pens.

Here's what Chordpro style looks like in detail:

> [D]Once she came in-[C]to my [D7]room,
> [Em]feathered hat, and [A]all,

If you look closely, you'll see square brackets around the capital letters indicating chord symbols. That's pretty much all you need to indicate which words are just words, and which ones are intended to be interpreted as chord symbols, resulting in this:

D   C   D7   Em   A
Once she came in-to my room, feathered hat, and all,

Neat, huh?

Now if your keyboard is like mine, you'll notice that your square bracket keys - [and] - actually have another set of symbols on top of them: meet { and }, the curly bracket. Just press the "Shift" key while pressing the [or] keys to bring up

their curvy siblings. In the Chordpro world, these curvy twins are actually used for labeling parts of a song, such as the title, subtitle, chorus, etc. Here is a sampling of what these shapely babies can do when they get their brackets around some easy-to-remember terms:
(source: http://tenbyten.com/software/songsgen/help/HtmlHelp/files_reference.htm)

> {title: title string} ({t:string})
> Specifies the title of the song. The title is used to sort the songs in the user interface. It appears at the top of the song, centered, and may be repeated if the song overflows onto a new column.
> {subtitle: subtitle string} ({su:string})
> Specifies a subtitle for the song. This string will be printed just below the title string.
> {start_of_chorus} ({soc})
> Indicates the start of a chorus. Songsheet Generator can apply a special marking to highlight the chorus, depending on the setting of the output destination. The marking is applied until the end_of_chorus directive appears.
> {end_of_chorus} ({eoc})
> Marks the end of a chorus.

Aack, are your eyes burning from reading raw code? I forgot to mention that "string" is computer-speak for "whatever you wanna type" – must've been the result of some bad pasta some poor programmer had after English class. Anyhow, if you were particularly hawk-eyed, you would've noticed that there were actually TWO versions of the code you could use – a longhand, and a shorthand version for lazy folks and those chronically addicted to texting. But enough of me translating babble-type – you'll probably learn more just by seeing and comparing the before and after of a Chordpro file:

Raw Chordpro example:

{title: Mary Had A Little Lamb}
{subtitle: A Shameless Exercise in Creating A Song In Chordpro Format}

[C]Mary had a little lamb, [G]Little lamb, [C]little lamb,
[C]Mary had a little lamb, Its [G]fleece was white as [C]snow.

{start_of_chorus}
[Eb7]Yeah, Baby, Yeah, Baby, [F]Yeah yeah yeah,
[Ab] Yeah, Baby, Yeah, Baby, [Bb]Woo woo woo!
{end_of_chorus}

Stunning result:

Mary Had A Little Lamb

A Shameless Exercise in Creating A Song In Chordpro Format

```
C              G       C
Mary had a little lamb, Little lamb, little lamb,
C                      G              C
Mary had a little lamb, Its fleece was white as snow.

Eb7                    F
Yeah, Baby, Yeah, Baby, Yeah yeah yeah,
Ab                     Bb
Yeah, Baby, Yeah, Baby, Woo woo woo!
```

To create your Chordpro masterpieces, all you need is to use a basic text editor, such as Notepad for Windows or TextEdit for Mac. You can even use a number of websites and apps for iPad and Android devices to create songs in the Chordpro format. Here is a sampling of some of the Chordpro-creating sites and apps:

Websites

WebChord

This is a free website to convert Chordpro and text files into prettified HTML files, suitable for printing. The above "Mary Had A Little Lamb" example was converted using this site. You can either enter the song manually in the provided text box, or upload a text file that contains your song – both methods require that you create your song using Chordpro commands.
http://webchord.sourceforge.net/

Chordpro.net

This is another Chordpro-to-HTML converter site. It includes a nifty graphic tablature feature showing how to finger the guitar chords used in your song. You need to enter the song directly into the text editor box using Chordpro lingo.

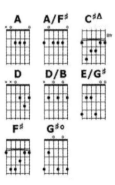

http://www.chordpro.net/Chordpro

Programs for Mac and PC

Chordsmith

This is a neat program that can convert text files into Chordpro files (and vice versa). It makes an attempt to recognize where the chords are aligned to the text and applies the Chordpro coding accordingly. Once it's in the Chordpro format, you can transpose to any key. Chordsmith is a Java-based program, meaning that you can install it on Mac and PC computers (and Linux ones as well, for you über-geeks out there). Best of all? It's "giftware" – meaning that it's free!

http://www.statistics101.net/chordsmith/

The SongCat Blog has an excellent tutorial on using Chordsmith.

http://appgen.com.au/blog/2012/06/25/how-to-create-chordpro-files/

Songsheet Generator

Songsheet Generator is another program for Mac and PC computers for creating Chordpro files from text files. It features some additional layout options, like having multiple columns or even multiple songs per page. You can even customize the background image for projecting your lyrics to a psychedelic audience!

Smog

```
A      Gn    Dm D
power sheep goat
A        Fm A Gn
who are you
Fm         D        A      Cn
From the outside looking in am i out of touch or
A    E    D E
who are you

smog

                                    A      E D E
nothing about you looks very different to me
mercy
        A        E      E
your chastity religion habits
Gn    Dsus2 Gn2    Dm4
have little to do with god
A         E
who do you serve
D         E
convenient god
A E    D E
no power so
A         E        D      E
god is great god is good
Gn    Dsus2 Gn2        Dm4
let us thank him for this food
A         G n E
amen then what

D             Dsus      E
nothing about you looks very different to me
no

christian-e / Corey Dettrman
Put Pretrid Laboratory
(C)1998 globalnervsystem
```

Yukionna

```
F
We have everything
Em7
We need nothing
A7    Dn Dm7
So rich
Ab
i hear a voice

Gr
I know your deeds greyscaler
C
I choke spit vomit

Ice so hot
Come embrace the fence
A grey zone home
Snow so warm

Asus4          E
He who has ears hear
Dm    C   Bb   Dm7
Lukewarm present Laodicea
Em7    Gr    r
Wake up remember greyscaler
Asus4            A
Wretched pitiful poor blind naked!
Em7          Gr F
Your time has come to die

Snow so warm
Ice so hot
Freeze your soul melt your life

The time has come
For remember to die
For greyscaler to die
To die

I hear a knocking at the door
Again a voice calls to my soul

Dm7    G7    Bb  F
Open the door overcome

christian-e
He equals death
(C)1998 globalnervsystem
```

Life and Works

The way I see it all there is

Look at my creation
It's my rendering of our Lord
Look at the emotion captured
Isn't it a fine image
You can almost feel the light the beauty

It won me int award
It's why I am renowned
Now I hope you can see now through my eyes now
My clever eyes now

It's art for the sake of art now
What other reasons do I need
I'll paint forever love me
It will last forever
My image never fails me

Oh the tears oh the thorns
What a sight
I know exactly what to do
I've seen it I just need to render it
I must do it do it now
He was weeping
He was bleeding
Like a fountain

christian-el / Corey Stelman
AgencyXEP
(C)1996 globalwavesystem

Smog

power sheep goat
who are you
from the outside looking in am i out of touch or
who are you

smog

nothing about you looks very different to me
mercy
your churchy religio-habits
have little to do with god
who do you serve
convenient god
no power no
god is great god is good
let us thank him for this food
amen then what

nothing about you looks very different to me
no

christian-el / Corey Stelman
Full Frontal Lobotomy
(C)1996 globalwavesystem

Wheel

Wheel

Clutching me into the great machine
Crushing me into the great machine

It will take me up
I will put my strength
It will use me up
I will have mind felt

I have been forced to revolve in the cultural revolution
Am revolving in the cultural revolution
I have chosen to revolve
Take me

As a good citizen you must not be anything
That is incorrect
That does not fit in
Sit right here imagine that you can contribute
Thank not want not
Life is good

Feel

christian-el
Lethal Injection
(C)1997 globalwavesystem

Commitment

Commitment
The hate of the world

I'm not taking it to heart
Not taking it to head
Or thorns or spear or cross
Not greater than my Master
Who paid the price
I should let them
Kill me in Jesus' name
Whom are they who
Kill me in Jesus' name

Commitment
The hate of the world
Should be raining on me
Should be hanging me on the cross
Should be raining on me
Should be hanging me on the cross
Set before me

Am i ready to die for you
Am i ready to die for you
Am i ready to die for you
Am i ready to die for you

If not committed not
Why not

To live in Christ to die to gain

christian-el
life equals death
(C)1993 globalwavesystem

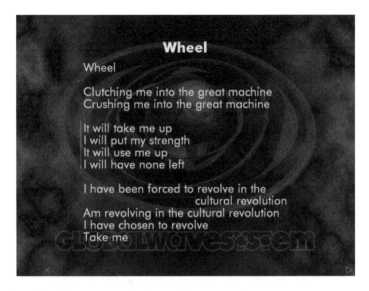

http://tenbyten.com/software/songsgen/

Apps for Tablets

OnSong for iOS

OnSong for iPad, iPhone, and iPod Touch is both a Chordpro/Text reader and editor. There are a ton of killer features, but the notable ones for this chapter are the ability to read, edit, and create Chordpro files.

http://onsongapp.com

Songbook by Linkesoft

Talk about covering your bases! Developer Linkesoft makes a family of programs and apps enabling users to read, edit, and write Chordpro files.

Windows PC users can use the SongBook Windows version: http://linkesoft.com/songbook/windows.html

Mac Users can use SongBook Mac: http://linkesoft.com/songbook/mac.html

iOS users (iPad, iPhone, iPod Touch) can use SongBook Chordpro for iOS: http://linkesoft.com/songbook/ios.html

Android users can use SongBook Android: http://linkesoft.com/songbook/android.html

As we've mentioned in previous chapters, you can explore many more text reader apps by feature sets and operating systems using AirTurn's interactive App Guide at http://airturn.com/appguide

CHAPTER THIRTY-THREE
Creating Music-Notation Content

For musicians working with traditional music notation – you know, the kind that introduced you to oxymoronic staff line acronyms like, "Every Good Boy Does Fine" – it's never been easier to scribe, produce, and instantly listen to your musical masterpieces in formats that look every bit as good as the ones produced by bigwig publishers.

And now, with the new ubiquity of tablets and computers among musicians, it's possible to completely bypass carbon pigment and mashed wood pulp – er, "ink" and "paper" – and instantly share copies of your latest opus to your choral members via Dropbox, extract parts for your chamber music ensemble lickity split, or listen to your music play itself back to check for missing accidentals in that fiendish new piano concerto you're about to unleash on those pesky prodigies at Juilliard.

Let's take a quick look at some of the major programs available for creating sheet music a la Beethoven, and then dive into an overview of the hardware tools you'll need to make your notes magically appear on the digital staff lines.

Note-by-Note Input

When Bach or Beethoven created their masterpieces, they dipped their respective quills into a jar of ink and laboriously scratched out their music onto parchment, one painstaking note at a time. For mainly classically trained composers, this is still the primary way to craft their compositions – the note-by-note part, I mean, not the quill and ink part. Fortunately, today's programs and hardware make this once arthritis-inducing method exponentially faster while still retaining the same creative thought process.

The two best-known – and most powerful – programs for writing note-by-note music in traditional notation are **Finale**, published by Make Music, and **Sibelius**, published by Avid. Finale, the senior digital denizen of the two, is generally praised for its rich feature set and extensive capabilities, while Sibelius won its legions of fans in large part due to its simplified interface and relative ease of use. Sorta like the ol' PC vs. Mac wars, eh? But I digress. Both programs are available for Mac and PC platforms and are excellent tools and vital for any serious musician. And even though digital playback of your scores with Finale or Sibelius' synthesized orchestral instruments won't win any recording contracts with Deutsche Grammaphone, it's still helpful as a reference point.

Finale and Sibelius

(As of this writing, Finale may end up being the last man standing, mainly due to financial uncertainties over Sibelius' parent company, Avid, which disbanded the Sibelius development team in late 2012. Case in point: Finale's publisher Make Music is actively developing a family of apps for reading Finale files on iPads, but Avid's own Sibelius reading app seems to be stuck in iOS 5 limbo, with serious incompatibilities with iOS 6. I'll be sure to update the tale – or demise - of Sibelius in the next edition of this book.)

An interesting open source option for creating note-by-note compositions is a program called **MuseScore**, which is available for Mac and PC users (www.musescore.org). Even though "open source" is computer lingo for "free," users will still find MuseScore to be adequate for most traditional music notation needs, particularly if don't need to fuss with advanced layouts or the ability to invent your own notation symbols (like you can in Finale and Sibelius). Just try not to crack your molars while listening to the teeth-clenching playback of your compositions using MuseScore's so-called digital "instruments." Hey, what do you expect for "free"?

Online Music Notation

With the advent of cloud-based computing – no, no, I don't mean hopping in a plane and flying around to draw smoke-trail messages in the sky – we're seeing a rise of applications that don't need to be installed in a computer. Rather, you access and use these programs through a web browser. The advantage of these types of programs is that you don't have to worry about checking for updates and installing patches to make sure you have the latest version, or losing your program (and all your hard work within that program) if your computer's hard drive decides to give itself a digital Hari-Kari and join the great cyber-graveyard in the digital ether.

This might seem a bit unsettling to composers who are used to having their compositions firmly under hand and quill, but think of it – just as you can buy music and download them into apps on a wide range of devices for reading them, or store your scores in online storage services like Dropbox, why not extend that capability to your latest magnum opus?

And think of the ease of sharing your scores with fellow performers, or sharing composition assignments in an online-classroom setting. Pulling the papyrus plug can suddenly free you to compose anywhere you can pick up a Wi-Fi internet connection, and not limit you to scrounging around for a No. 2 with an intact sharpened point or an eraser that hasn't been mummified into a rock-hard door stop, much less searching for a blank piece of manuscript paper. Here are a few online music-notation services that offer free trials for a limited number of stored compositions and paid subscriptions for an unlimited library and expanded feature sets.

Noteflight

This HTML-5 coded service seamlessly integrates web-based composing with online sharing and collaboration, making it ideal for using this in a virtual classroom or musical-ensemble setting. With the full subscription, teachers can even create their own custom web pages and share assignments to their select group of students. The composition tools are quite extensive surprisingly full-featured. Here's a little ditty I worked on to show off some of Noteflight's compositional capabilities:

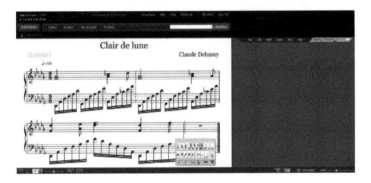

Noteflight files can be printed directly to a printer, or exported in MusicXML and MIDI formats for use in other music-notation programs and readers, and you can even create audio WAV files to listen to a computerized performance of your musical creations.

Since Noteflight is an HTML-5 based website, it is fully compatible with Safari browsers on iOS devices like the iPad. The website will detect the iOS device and show a custom view that is much more finger-friendly, with the inclusion of a handy virtual piano for entering notes on the fly. As a nifty little bonus, you can even turn "pages" hands free within the website using a page-turning pedal like the AirTurn BT-105 (see Chapter 35, "Controllers").

www.noteflight.com

Scorio

Scorio is another web-based music-notation service that offers various tiers of subscriptions. Its web editor is not as full-featured as Noteflight's, but it does offer an intriguing service for converting PDF files into music notation that can be edited. I tried the service with one of my scanned PDF scores, but the file never got processed. Perhaps my scan was too messy? I suspect that you would need a score that is pristinely scanned, and ideally not marred with any pencil or ink markings whatsoever. If it actually works, that would be a handy service in and of itself...oh well, hope springs eternal. Back to the music notation part...

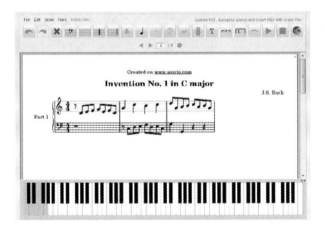

You can either click on the staff lines and spaces to enter notes, or use the handy onscreen keyboard to "play" your note entries. As I mentioned, the notation-input options are rather limited, and perhaps best suited for students learning the rudimentaries of music notation. I originally wanted to create an example with an incomplete measure in the beginning, but I couldn't for the life of me figure out how to do this, so I reverted to a simpler example.

www.scorio.com

Score also has an "app" for the iPad called <u>Music Case</u>, but it's not a standalone app per se – it's just a glorified web browser for creating compositions with the Scorio web service. Like Noteflight working through the Safari browser, you need an active web connection to create your compositions.

The virtual keyboard can be slid in either direction to make it easier to enter in notes that are higher/lower in the scale (note the green arrows on the bottom of the iPad screen). Scorio files can be exported as MusicXML, MIDI, and LilyPond files (ah, LilyPond...that's an open-source music-notation program for Mac, PC, and Linux that's billed as the best tool for the most beautiful rendition of music that approaches the quality of professionally engraved manuscripts, but it is a total bear to work with as you have to enter in every single detail via an obtuse programming code. See, take a look –

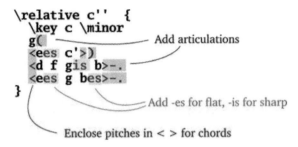

```
\relative c'' {
  \key c \minor
  g(                          Add articulations
  <ees c'>)
  <d f gis b>-.
  <ees g bes>-.
}
                              Add -es for flat, -is for sharp

              Enclose pitches in < > for chords
```

Egads, pretty ugly, eh? And quite a bit beyond the scope of this book, but if you really want to explore this fascinating migraine-inducing method of digital-music notation, please be my guest and visit http://www.lilypond.org/)

Free-Play Notation

Are you one of those whiz-bang musicians who can play by ear but can't make out a treble clef from a 64th note? Never fear, you counterpoint cop-outs – today's technologies make it as easy to notate your improvised riffs as it is to tell Siri call up your favorite playlist (easier, actually – Siri's voice-recognition capabilities can be laughably woeful at times). I like to call this next batch of programs "free-play notation software." The idea is to hook up a musical instrument that the computer can recognize (keyboards are the most common, but there are ways to get guitars connected as well), set your tempo like a metronome, and play to your heart's content. The computer will automatically take care of rhythmic placement, accidentals, and all the other stuff that you probably slept through while trying to drudge through that music-theory book.

And lest you think that such "writing by riffing" is akin to "compositional cheating," here's a story that hopefully shows the benefit of this method of notation:

One summer, I invited a good friend of mine – Jeffrey Khaner, principle flutist of the Philadelphia Orchestra – to perform a recital together with me at the cavernous Great Auditorium in the quaint beachside resort town of Ocean Grove, New Jersey. Jeff agreed to do so on one condition: he wanted me to write arrangements of two Jazz tunes for him, "Black Coffee" and "Angel Eyes." I found this to be a rather odd request, since we were both classical musicians and neither of us played Jazz. The extent of my Jazz playing was filling in for the Jazz Band way back in elementary school and flailing around at my attempts to sight read handwritten scores. Jeff handed me a CD of Ella Fitzgerald singing some classics and hoped that I could come up with something that would make him sound like Ella. Tall order, but I shrugged, fired up my copy of Sibelius, and did my best to come up with something that sounded as "jazz-like" as my virgin classical ears could muster.

We played the two arrangements as encores, and Jeff liked them so much he remarked, "We should record some of this stuff." I took the compliment in stride and proceeded to completely forget about it. A few months later as the fall semester was in full stride at Curtis and the holidays were approaching, Jeff gave me one of his inquisitive arched eyebrows and asked, "So, where's the music?"

"The music for what?" I replied, perplexed.

"The Jazz album!" he almost roared. "We're getting ready to record in a month! I have the hall and the engineer already booked!"

Jazz album? I was flabbergasted. I had thought he was just making a comment in passing – I didn't think he was actually *serious* about recording a whole album of these half-baked arrangements! Panicked, I quarantined myself in front of my computer, cobbled together a couple of sketches in a matter of days, and brought the printed copies to our first rehearsal the following week. We played through the first song, then Jeff lowered his flute, the disdain coloring his face like prune juice in a glass of milk.

"This sucks," he eloquently proclaimed. I sat at the piano, dumbfounded. I asked him to try to articulate what he was looking for, what was missing, *anything* to give me a clue how to turn this musical train wreck into something less catastrophic.

"This just sounds too stiff. It doesn't sound like *you!*"

Sound like me? What in the world did he mean?

"You know, the way you doodle at the piano whenever you're accompanying a student during lesson breaks."

I had a bad habit of plunking out funny chords to emphasize the punch line of a joke, or mindlessly spilling out improvised riffs while waiting for a lesson to start. I never thought in a million years that these unconscious finger spasms would actually turn out to be something worth listening to. But then, a light bulb went on in my brain.

I had approached the project using a traditional note-by-note approach. That evening, I ditched Sibelius and fired up a different program instead: **Sonar**, published by Cakewalk. Sonar was designed mainly for digital audio production, but it had a neat feature where notes could appear either as dots on a piano roll, or as traditional music notation, even though it wasn't designed as a compositional tool in that sense. I started by playing out the main melody – Jeff's part –using my digital keyboard and Sonar to record that part on the top track. I then created a new piano track, started the solo track above, and let myself go – I improvised as I "accompanied" the solo line. Then, I muted that piano track, created another one, and improvised again.

I did this several times until I felt like I had captured some good ideas. I then opened up all the tracks in the traditional notation view, then cherry picked the best measures from among all the takes. The result? The "ultimate" improv, culled from the best amalgam of all the takes.

The next day, I took this new version into my rehearsal with Jeff. After playing it through, a broad smile crept over his face. *This* was exactly what he had been looking for. The music had a natural, freely improvised feel, capturing what my ears and fingers felt far better than what my compositional brain had tried to meticulously craft. And with that, I was able to quickly "write out" all the rest of the arrangements in plenty of time for our recording sessions, with the music sounding about as close to "jazz" as I could muster, all thanks to a shift from note-by-note writing to free-play notation, thanks to the wonders of digital technology.

Free-Play Notation Software

I've already mentioned Sonar in my little story above – it's available for Mac and PC (http://www.cakewalk.com/Products/SONAR/X2-Producer/default.aspx) – but let's touch on some other free-play music notation programs that specifically translate your free-form improvisations into musical notation that can be read and performed note for note.

GarageBand for Mac

This gateway program is both easy to use and surprisingly powerful for a fraction of the cost of many other high-octane music creation programs. While it's primarily intended as a program for exploring, playing, and recording musical creations using dozens of digital representations of real instruments, its music notation feature does a pretty good job of rendering what you play, depending on the rhythmic complexity of your compositions. If you're playing something with a basic "beat," the default settings should work fine. If you're riffing something at a speed that causes the keys to melt from the blazing friction, you'll want to make sure you quantize the note values to a small-enough value to capture as much as possible without jamming them into broken "chords."

Keep in mind that GarageBand for iOS does not yet have the option to output your music into traditional notation – you're left to juggle floating bars representing the notes and their time values, something akin to the holes in the old fashioned piano rolls that were so popular around the turn of the 20th century.

http://www.apple.com/ilife/garageband/

Progression 2.0 by Notion Music

Progression v. 2 is an example of music notation software for Mac and PC that is specifically geared for guitar players. It features the ability to create tablature, as well as standard lead sheets and traditional music notation.

http://www.notionmusic.com/products/progression2.html

Guitar Pro 6

Guitar Pro 6 for Mac and PC computers is optimized for use with the Fretlight line of electric guitars (http://fretlight.com/). Fretlight guitars feature an innovative LED lighting system on the polymer fretboard, mainly intended to help players learn chords and scales by showing where the notes are with the use of dynamic lights. The innovative "improvise" feature shows notes that can be used in any given scale mode, inviting players to jam along with backing tracks for true free-play exploration and composition. Music can be written in tablature, chord chart, and traditional music notation formats.

http://www.guitar-pro.com/en/index.php

268

MIDI Hardware

So – much like the question of how to get your sheet music into your computer – how do you get your computer to capture your music from your keyboard or guitar?

There are three basic hardware components to creating digital music notation, and they all center around an old electronic protocol called MIDI, which is short for Musical Instrument Digital Interface. Developed in the early 1980s, MIDI is the most universal format for getting computers to understand what musical instruments are saying, from the pitch of the note to its length and volume and several other parameters. To start, you will need an instrument that has the ability to speak MIDI. Sorry, that rules out just about anything without an electric cord. The most prolific MIDI instruments around are digital keyboards, and you'll be able to determine this by looking for at least one (usually at least two) large ports with some funny little holes inside that follow this pattern:

When MIDI ports come in pairs, one of them will be labeled "out," the other will be labeled "in" (and some instruments will have a "thru" MIDI port, but we don't need to worry about that in the context of this book). You will need a MIDI cable to connect one end to the MIDI OUT port.

As for the other end? Ah, that takes us to the second hardware component: the digital MIDI interface.

These interfaces will take all shapes and sizes, but at their most basic, they will provide ports for your MIDI cable to connect to on one end, and on the other end some way to connect to your computer – these days, it will be some sort of USB cable. The cable that came OUT of your MIDI instrument? The other end will go into the IN port of your MIDI interface. If you can get that picture into your head – music coming OUT of your instrument and IN-to your computer – then you'll always remember which end of the MIDI cable to plug into which port on whichever device.

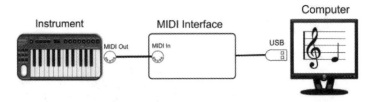

Here's a quick look at some MIDI interface options for Mac and PC computers:

M-Audio UNO 1x1 USB MIDI Interface

The USB Uno provides a simple, extremely inexpensive solution for connecting MIDI devices to USB-based-(Mac 8.6 or greater) and PC- (Windows 98, ME, 2000 and XP) computers. The compact injection-molded unit features built-in extension cables that simplify connections for novices. Uno also features MIDI activity indicators for each port. The unit is self-powered, thereby eliminating the need for yet another "wall wart" power supply and making it ideal for mobile use with laptops.

M-Audio USB MIDISport 1x1

This one-in, one-out M-Audio USB MIDI audio interface transfers 16 x 16 MIDI channels. It connects to any USB-equipped PC or Mac computer (Windows 98 or Mac OS 8.6) and requires no external power supply. The M-Audio USB

MIDI interface's compact size facilitates use with laptop and notebook computers. Installation is a breeze — no computer disassembly; no jumpers to set; no I/O addresses, IRQs, or DMA channels to configure. Just plug it in. PC/Mac.

M-Audio Fast Track Pro (no longer in production)

I used this model for many years, and it still has a place next to my piano whenever I need to write music or record MIDI files. This is a great example of an interface box that includes XLR inputs for semi-pro and pro microphones (the ones that use three pins to connect) USB Audio Interface and MIDI Interface with two Phantom-powered Microphone/Line Inputs.

(**Note:** some keyboards and guitars (such as the Fretlight guitars mentioned above in the Guitar Pro software section) are built with a direct-to-computer USB MIDI interface, so that you can skip the hardware interface. Well, lah-dee-dah for you if you have one! That just means a bunch of software drivers you'll need to install into your computer to understand the connection, but you can usually find links to those from the website of your keyboard/instrument manufacturer.)

In the case of the iPad, which so conveniently obliterated the need for standard USB cables, you will need to get a special "made for iPad" MIDI interface. Again, these come in all shapes and sizes, from simple cables to the 30-pin port, to whiz-bang control boxes that you can slide your iPad into. Note that with Apple's headlong rush into innovation/obsolescence, the 30-pin adapters that were ubiquitous features of the first three generations of iPads and iPhones up to the iPhone 4S have bitten the dust, and you'll need to look for Lightning Port MIDI adapters if you bought that shiny new iPad 4 or iPad Mini...sigh...

The third hardware component is – naturally – the computer. As we discussed before, your choice of software will, in most cases, determine your choice of computer. Or if you're stuck with a given computer, then the egg will have to determine the chicken, or something along those lines. In any case, hopefully you see how vital the software/hardware relationship is in terms of the options available to you.   Mac and PC users currently have the widest options, while tablet users are much more limited when it comes to creating digital sheet music with MIDI instruments (frankly, I don't even know of any MIDI interface/ software options for Android tablet users ... what a shame.)

And then there was iPad ...

MIDI interfaces for tablets – er, the iPad – are most popularly used to control virtual instrument apps and make cool sounds come out of them. Sadly, there really aren't that many music-notation apps taking advantage of MIDI input. The only one currently available in the App store is called **Notion** (http://www.notionmusic.com/products/notionipad.html), although there are more apps sure to come, such as a fascinating **Kickstarter** project from ThinkMusic that will give you the ability to draw music notation by hand with a special stylus from Adonit (http://www.kickstarter.com/projects/thinkmusictech/thinkmusic-ipad-app-the-ultimate-music-notation-ap). Note that you don't need a MIDI instrument to write music in Notion – you can compose notes directly with the touch of a finger, albeit the note-by-note way to the extreme. Adding a MIDI instrument obviously makes note entry a lot faster.

As for the hardware side of things – MIDI interfaces for the iPad – there are plenty of 30-pin options for the older iPads (1, 2, and 3), and more in development for the latest iPads and other iOS devices (iPhone, iPod Touch) with Lightning connectors. Here is a quick look at some of the options currently available:

IK Multimedia's iRig MIDI

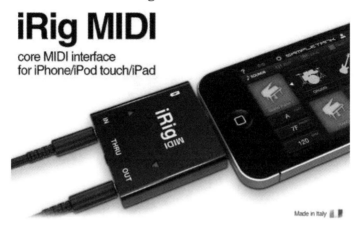

This is a compact MIDI interface for iOS devices (iPhones, iPod Touches, and iPads) with 30-pin connectors. The iRig MIDI comes with two 1.6m/5.2' cables that connect to standard MIDI cables to attach to your MIDI-ready instrument. Works with any app compatible with the CoreMIDI protocol, which includes apps such as GarageBand and the like.

Line 6 MIDI Mobilizer II

The Line 6 MIDI Mobilizer II is another 30-pin MIDI interface for iOS devices similar to the iRig MIDI device above.

Yamaha i-MX1

Ditto for the Yamaha i-MX1, but without the pretty blinky lights.

Alesis iO Dock

This is a heavy-duty, all-in-one, 30-pin audio interface for your iPad, featuring balanced XLR and quarter inch inputs and outputs, as well as USB and standard MIDI connectors. If you're going to be serious about using your iPad for composing and recording pro-level audio, you should take a serious look at this puppy. Lightning-port version for the newer iPads coming, I presume.

MIDI Interfaces for Acoustic Instruments

While most composers work with digital keyboards or synthesizers that are MIDI-capable with MIDI ports built in, here are some interesting alternatives for those who want to compose using acoustic instruments.

Roland GK-3

If you don't have a guitar with a built-in MIDI interface like the Fretlight guitar (www.fretlight.com), you can add on an external MIDI pickup like the Roland GK-3.

QRS PNOscan II Acoustic Piano MIDI strip

Want the best of both worlds? The sound and touch of an acoustic piano with the computer brains of a MIDI interface? Thanks to an optical MIDI strip called the PNOscan II from QRS, now you can! Installation isn't for the faint of heart, so you might want to consult your local piano dealer to see if they can retrofit your instrument, or see if they offer pianos with MIDI strips pre-installed, like the next device we'll look at.

PianoDisc QuietTime GT-2S

PianoDisc is one of the world's leading manufacturers of digital player-piano systems. They provide a neat system called QuietTime that features a rail to stop the piano hammers just shy of the strings, and a GT-2S MIDI strip that will capture keyboard and pedal activities for MIDI output with the QuietTime rail on or off. That way you can compose or listen to a digital output of your musical musings late into the night without disturbing anyone, or play with the full inspiration of acoustic bliss while simultaneously outputting your performance to your favorite notation program. QuietTime and GT-2S systems will need to be installed by your friendly neighborhood (and PianoDisc-authorized) piano dealer.

CHAPTER THIRTY-FOUR

Containers: Transforming a Digital Reader Into a Music Stand

Ah, the venerable music stand! Since its ancient Chinese origins from 200 B.C. to its late 14th century popularization by German and Swiss composers, the music stand is to musicians what butter is to bread (or salsa to tortillas for my vegan and gluten-free friends). And while these ancient podiums are certainly capable of holding the new digital tools for reading music, they possess one fatal design flaw: the "beer bump." You know, the accidental nudge from a rowdy band mate, or a passionate bow arm that turns a sheaf of manuscript paper into an embarrassing display of floor flotsam, or turns a $500 tablet into a really expensive metal and broken-glass doorstop. If you're a mobile musician who needs to prop his music on a freestanding platform weighing less than 500 pounds (i.e., acoustic grand pianos and pipe organs), then you're going to want to invest in a container that can safely support your digital investment while giving you an optimal view of your music. And hey, it doesn't hurt to get something that looks cool on stage at the same time!

The venerable Manhasset Music Stand,
a fixture of every cluttered band room

iPad users have it great, thanks to its incredible popularity and the mostly uniform design of the iPad's dimensions throughout its development (notable exceptions being the original iPad, which is thicker than its progeny, and the diminutive iPad Mini). You'll find a dizzying array of mount and stand options for the iPad in all shapes, sizes, and functions. But non-iPad tablet users needn't despair – there is a new class of universal tablet mounts that provide mounting options for them as well. Even smartphone users can enjoy some slick mounting options if they want to show off the acuity of their latest Lasik eye surgery. And folks who use laptop computers also have some cool mounting solutions, which we'll look at towards the end of this chapter.

Tablet Mounts

With Apple churning out a new i-Device every six months, and other tablet makers constantly gorging the market with a plethora of iPad wannabe's, it's impossible to point to any single container as the ultimate digital-music-stand solution. With that in mind, I'd like to suggest six key features to consider when shopping for your Manhasset makeover, broken down into **three T's** and **three C's**:

Three T's: Tilt, Turn, and Topple

Tilt

Does your mount give you the option to easily tilt the screen to accommodate a variety of views? A seated musician will need a more upright tilt. A standing or taller musician might need a steeper angle. Add in pesky stage lights and you'll appreciate a tablet mount that can adjust its viewing angle to ward off screen glare.

Turn

Many music-reading apps give users the option to view their music in portrait (full-page, upright screen) or landscape (half the music page, horizontal screen) modes. While portrait mode may be the default way to see an entire page at a time, you may want to turn your tablet on its side in case you want an enlarged view, a half page at a time. If you find yourself doing this frequently, you'll want to consider a mount that can turn easily between portrait and landscape views. Keep in mind that the more knobs and screws you have to fiddle with to get the angle just right while keeping a safe grip on your tablet, the bigger the hassle. The **iKlip** from IK Multimedia is a very popular iPad mount, but choose your tilt carefully – it's notoriously difficult to switch from portrait to landscape views once you have it clamped in place.

The iKlip from IK Multimedia

While some mounts provide a ball bearing to turn your tablet at any rotation angle, other mounts provide a nice tactile click to help you quickly position your tablet into an optimal portrait or landscape position. The **K&M iPad Mic Mount** provides this sort of portrait- and landscape-view tactile click.

The K&M 19710 iPad Mic Mount

Topple

If your tablet mount comes as an all-in-one stand solution (as opposed to a mount that attaches onto an existing stand, such as a mic stand), you'll want to make sure it isn't susceptible to the "beer bump." No stand is perfectly impervious to a tussle with an inebriated musician or a burst of gale-force winds, but a good stand should offer some level of stability and protection from the occasional love tap and slanted concert stage (old acoustic halls are slightly slanted for optimal sound projection – check out the main stage at Carnegie Hall if you can get past the army of stage-hand security).

As a general rule of thumb, the wider the base of the stand, the more stable it will be. Tripods tend to be more stable overall than circular mounts, but even then quality of build will be a major factor in their stability (ask any owner of a cheap wire-frame music stand). The **Peak iPad Floor Stand** is a cheap option for budget-conscious musicians, but it's particularly prone to tipsy troubadours, due to its flimsy build and narrow tripod spread.

The Peak iPad Music Stand

Three C's: Clothed, Clip, and Carry

Clothed

Bare or bound? By that question, I mean, does your tablet accompany you like a hippie at a nudist colony, or do you have it hermetically sealed in a Kevlar case designed to withstand snapped guitar strings, flying drum sticks, and coffee spills? If your case makes it easy to pop your tablet in and out, then working with a tablet mount designed for bare tablets won't be much of an issue. If, on the other hand, your case requires a combination code, two keys and three screwdrivers to pry free, then you'll want to find a mount that can accommodate your obsession for protection.

The OtterBox is one of the toughest – and bulkiest – cases on the market

Most iPad music-stand mounts are designed for iPads in their birthday suit. A form-fitted mount will offer the most secure support when attached to a stand. But if you insist on maintaining a modicum of modesty for your iPad or are using a non-iPad tablet, then you'll want to consider a universal mount/ stand for your tablet.

The Joy Factory's Universal Tablet Mount
for Tripods and Mic Stands

Keep in mind the irony of tablet protection: the thicker your suit of tablet armor, the more difficult it may be to securely affix it to a mount or stand, depending on the weight, girth, and texture of the tablet case. As with the "beer bump" test for Topple, you'll want to see if your universal mount is susceptible to the "slip test." That is, when you rotate the tablet, how prone will it be to slip out of the mount's grip? The CastIV Tab Station is an example of a universal mount that only grips two sides of a tablet. If the tablet is too heavy or slippery and the mount is rotated with the tabs holding only the sides, the spring-loaded tabs can lose their grip and send your tablet into an unexpected drop-test zone.

The CastIV Tab Station Universal Tablet Mount

Lest you Otterbox-toting tablet troubadours despair, AirTurn has come up with an innovative approach to the universal tablet-mounting problem. Modeled after the way two human hands and fingers grip and hold a tablet, the AirTurn Manos Mount features two heavy-duty spring arms with unique rubberized "finger grips" that can hold anything from a smartphone to an Otterbox-ensconced iPad with the security of a New York fashionista gripping her latest Gucci bag acquisition. The AirTurn Manos Mount can rotate into locked positions for portrait and landscape views.

The AirTurn Manos Mount

The AirTurn Manos Mount – not just for tablets!

Clip

If you're tired of having a forest of stands on stage, you'll want to consider clipping options for your tablet mount. If your mount can attach to a standard mic-stand screw, then you can take advantage of both standard mic stands and side-mount attachment options so that you can use one stand to hold both your tablet and a microphone, for example. Here is one such configuration available from TheGigEasy for iPads.

The GigEasy iPad mount, attached to a side mount

If you're considering an all-in-one mount and stand, you'll want to look at the shape of the stand itself to see if it can accommodate side-mount attachments. In order to attach these, either a cylindrical or straight edge is required. The **Z3 iPad stand** by Rat Stands, for example, has beveled edges, making it a slick-looking stand on its own, but next to impossible to affix a side clamp.

Rat Stands' Z3 iPad Stand

Carry

If you're a musician who plays in various locations, you'll want to consider how easy it is to carry your tablet mount or stand. If you regularly encounter mic stands wherever you work, then you can probably get by with just having the mount itself in your gig bag. If mic stands aren't as common in your line of musical work (Classical musicians rarely encounter mic stands, for example – they often get incensed if they're asked to electronically amplify their acoustic instruments, believe it or not!), then you'll want to consider either a collapsible all-in-one mount and stand solution, or find a separate portable mic or tripod stand to accompany the tablet mount (the use of a tripod or mic stand depends on the type of fitting on your mount). Just keep in mind your height requirements – do you play standing or sitting? Does your head bump into a basketball rim, or can you stretch out comfortably in a cramped coach-class airplane seat?

Of course, other considerations will be bulk and weight. For example, the **Flote Tablet Stand** is a beautiful design, but it probably won't fit in the overhead luggage bin:

293

The Flote Tablet Stand

If you have a mic-stand-ready tablet mount, then you might want to consider getting a compact collapsible mic stand like this **Concertino**, and supplementing it with a gooseneck if you need the extra height.

Gooseneck and Mic Stand Concertino

*Gooseneck, Mic Stand Concertino,
and TheGigEasy iPad Mount assembled*

Smartphone Mounts

Aside from the AirTurn Manos Mount, another interesting option for guitar and bass players is a smartphone mount that clamps directly onto your instrument. **Sonic Clamp** makes a pressure clamp that can mount your iPhone or iPod Touch along the rim or the body of your favorite fretted friend. If you don't mind reading chord charts off of a diminutive screen, this can be a great way to make it look like you actually know what you're playing without the big giveaway of a large tablet screen blocking your moussed up coiffure. A universal phone mount is coming soon from the Sonic Clamp guys (www.sonicclamp.com).

The Sonic Clamp for iPhone and iPad Touch

A Sonic Clamp doing double duty

Laptop Stands

Tablets, schmablets — you've stubbornly eschewed the craze over lightweight, supermodel-thin slabs of metal and glass with time-defying battery life in favor of your tried and trusty laptop. Fortunately for you, you grizzled digital sea hag, you can still mount your laptop as a "music stand" in safety and style. Laptop tripods are essentially portable tables that feature collapsible legs and bodies and tabletops that can be detached. Some laptop tripods feature "beer bump" protection in the form of a rubber coating that grips the laptop surprisingly well even at extreme angles. One such manufacturer of laptop tripods is a company called **insTand**. It features both lightweight and heavy-duty chrome versions.

The insTand CR3 lightweight laptop tripod

The insTand CR5 heavy-duty chrome laptop tripod

CHAPTER THIRTY-FIVE

Controllers: Expanding Ways to Work With Your Computer

For the digital-sheet-music musician, we will be concerned about two primary types of controllers: hands-free page turners, and devices for drawing ink markings on a digital page.

A Page-Turner's Tale

When I first discovered the world of using computers to read sheet music, I was in digital – and musical – nirvana. I was amazed at the clarity of the notes on my Toshiba Tablet PC and the ease of making markings with a digital pen that felt like a smooth Mont Blanc. The idea of being able to, one day, carry *all* my hundreds of paper scores in a single device was something bordering on magical. And yet, there was one potentially fatal flaw in this miraculous setup: how to turn the page? The backlit screen only gave me half a window into my customary two-page open-book world by displaying a single page of music at a time. I needed to find a way to extend the magic of virtual sheet music to incorporate a really cool way to turn digital pages *hands free*.

My first thought was to find a programmable pedal that could send a "page down" keyboard command to my computer with the tap of my foot so that I could keep playing with my hands uninterrupted. Back in 2002, there was no shortage of industrial foot switches, but they all had one or more serious drawbacks:

- They were bulky
- They made an audible clicking sound (not a concern for high octane rock 'n' roll music, perhaps, but a serious faux pas when it came to performing in a pristine acoustic setting as a classical pianist)
- They required an unsightly USB cable connection (hey, I wanted to look cool on stage, not emphasize my geeky dorkdom by having cables trail off the side of my piano!)
- They were difficult to program (one of my secret fears was that the USB might get accidentally

disconnected in transit from Green Room to stage – doing so would require me to reboot the computer and reprogram the pedals to send the correct commands. And the programming was klunky to begin with!)

The first pedal I worked with was a programmable three-pedal transcription device made by X-keys. Definitely fell under the bulky, audible, unsightly, and hard-to-program categories. On top of that, I discovered that pressing the right button (the one I assigned to turn pages forwards) too hard would cause it to get stuck under the plastic housing!

The X-Keys button programmable foot pedal

The next pedal I experimented with was a Delcom Engineering foot switch. At least it was considerably smaller than my X-keys pedal, but it still had an ugly USB cable and clicked so loudly I once considered trying to bury it under a mound of carpeting during a recording session!

Delcom Engineering's clackity pedal

In 2006, I came across a Korean company that made the first wireless pedal for turning pages – the FP-1. Huzzah, huzzah! I thought I had found the holy grail! Compact, silent, wireless, no need to program anything – this thing was the bomb!

Musebook's FP-1 wireless pedal

"Bomb" was too descriptive a term, I soon discovered. This thing bombed all right – right in the middle of a hair-raising rendition of Shostakovich's blazing fast 2nd Violin Concerto's second movement! It turned out that the radio frequency transmitted by the pedal was actually bouncing off the bottom of the dense keyboard of the concert grand I was performing with, resulting in intermittent page turns and buckets of sweat as I frantically stomped my foot and pulled out my digital pen to manually maneuver the page turns. Lesson learned: 90 percent reliability just doesn't cut it when it comes to using a page turner in a high-pressure performance situation! Little surprise that the company went out of business a year or so later, and the ridiculously overpriced wireless pedal never materialized on USA shores.

I then began to experiment with a neat device from Griffin called the PowerMate. This was a device designed as a rotating control knob – any movement, from rotating left or right, or pressing the PowerMate as a near-silent button, could be assigned any keyboard function. Plus it had a wicked cool glowing blue light on the bottom, offsetting the lanky USB cable still required to control the host computer.

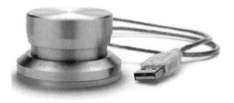

Griffin's PowerMate

Problem was, it was designed to be used by a hand on a flat tabletop, not as a foot pedal. In an attempt to increase the reliability of using the PowerMate as a foot switch, I tried building a number of cradles to provide an offset angle to better accommodate the action of a foot press – first out of wood and clay:

A wooden and clay cradle for my PowerMate

Then solely out of a clay-like substance called "Sculpey," designed to be hard-fired in a conventional home oven:

A Sculpey cradle for my PowerMate

Alas, these half-baked ideas still resulted in a page-turning foot pedal that fell short of 100 percent reliability – there were still occasional blanks whenever I tried to fire off a page turn, enough so that I found myself constantly praying that the page would actually turn and walking off stage after a 50-page concerto that left my stomach in knots and the Pepto-Bismol company happily soaring in stock price.

In 2008, I was officially fed up with trying to jury-rig off-the-shelf products to fit my needs, and went into business with my entrepreneurial mentor and engineering guru Lester Karplus. Together, we determined to build our own page-turning pedal with three essential qualities:

- It had to be silent.
- It had to be sleek.
- It had to be simple.

It had to be silent: no more clicks, squeaks, or any distracting audible properties that could detract from a blissful moment of Debussyean pianissimo or a Grammy award-winning engineer's hyper-sensitive K&M microphones – I wanted the ultimately silent pedal.

It had to be sleek: no more wires. I wanted wireless, Baby. And the more compact the package, the better – something that could slip easily into the side pocket of a laptop bag would be ideal.

It had to be simple: no more manually assigning keyboard commands to button function A or B, no more reboots to clear an accidentally disconnected cable – I wanted to turn the pedal on and go. Easy peasy.

The result? **The AirTurn AT-104** wireless page-turning transmitter with USB receiver dongle.

The AirTurn AT-104 wireless USB page turner

This puppy was designed to work with a wide variety of momentary switches – we settled on bundling it with the Boss FS-5U foot switches, the quietest ones we could find on the market.

The AT-104 with two Boss FS-5U foot switches

Plug the USB receiver into any Mac or PC USB port, and voila – instant page turner. No need to program or configure anything. The AT-104 would transmit either a "Page Down" or a "Page Up" command wirelessly, depending on which attached pedal was pressed.

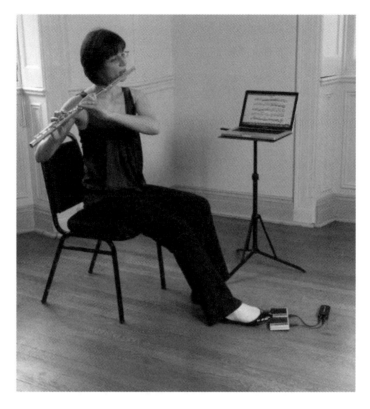

A musician using a MacBook to read music, and an AirTurn
AT-104 with Boss FS-5U pedals to turn pages hands free

We had developed what we thought was the ultimate page-turning pedal, but alas, the rest of the world still wasn't sold on the idea of using computers to read music. Unless you bought an expensive Windows-based Tablet PC, you could only practically read music half a page at a time on the landscape screens of most laptops. Then two years later, Apple laid the golden egg in the form of the iPad.

Even though Amazon introduced the world to the idea of using tablets to read books in 2007 with its groundbreaking Kindle, it wasn't until the introduction of the iPad that digital reading went into hyperdrive. But there was a new problem with the iPad: there was no friggin' USB port! Steve Jobs had determined that the iPad was going to be a finger-centric device. No more pens (styluses, in computer-speak), no more keyboards, and as the AT-104 was essentially a wireless keyboard with two keys, it was completely incompatible with the iPad. The world was going two steps forward and one serious step back when it came to reading books digitally – you still had to use a finger to swipe the page, mimicking the action of paper books. So much for hands free page turning, right?

Back to the Drawing Board

The lack of a USB port forced us to rethink a way to work with devices like the iPad. Fortunately, the iPad was equipped with a hobbled version of Bluetooth, a wireless protocol that's most popularly used to connect earpieces with smart phones, transforming digital denizens into folks babbling one-sided monologues with invisible friends. The result was the AirTurn BT-105, a Bluetooth page-turning transceiver, and an amazing collaboration with more than 150 programmers worldwide that helped to incorporate BT-105 into their iPad (and iPhone and iPod Touch) apps.

The AirTurn BT-105 Bluetooth page-turning transceiver

Like the AT-104, the AirTurn BT-105 was designed to be controlled by any momentary normally open (NO) switch. We first started offering the BT-105 with the Boss FS-5U foot switches, just as we had done with the AT-104.

A BT-105 with two Boss FS-5U switches

Thanks to the incredible popularity of the iPad, the BT-105 sold like hotcakes. But despite the BT-105's popularity, one thing bothered us. Even though the Boss FS-5U foot switches were great pedals, they weren't *absolutely* silent – there were no clicks per se, but you could still hear an occasional squeak or mechanical rattle. These things were designed to be stage sturdy, not acoustic prima donnas.

We decided to take a crack at designing our own foot pedal from scratch, one that would be as sturdy as the Boss FS-5U while being truly and unequivocally silent. The result was the ATFS pedal, now in its second iteration as the ATFS-2.

The AirTurn ATFS silent pedal

What makes the ATFS-2 so unique is what it lacks: no switch, no springs, and no moving mechanical parts (aside from the molded hinge). With nothing to rub against, you have the most silent switch in the consumer market to date.

Look, Ma ... no mechanics!

For musicians who like an "all-in-one" page-turning solution, the AirTurn BT-105 is available with two ATFS-2 pedals affixed to a pedal board.

The BT-105 with two ATFS-2 silent pedals on a pedal board

For musicians who want more flexibility in placing their page-turning pedals closer or further apart, the BT-105 is available with ATFS-2 pedals sans pedal board:

The BT-105 with two ATFS-2 silent pedals without a pedal board

The More the Merrier

For most musicians, two pedals are perfectly adequate – one pedal to turn pages forwards, the other to turn pages backwards. What more could a digital-sheet-music reader need?

In November of 2012, at the request of several developers, we came out with a four-pedal version of the AirTurn BT-105.

The AirTurn BT-105 with four ATFS-2 pedals

Thanks to the ingenuity of some of these developers, users could now add several new ways to control their sheet music, wirelessly and hands free. In addition to turning pages forwards and backwards, users could navigate between songs in a set list, or assign a pedal to toggle on an audio backing track, or even assign pedals to transpose music into different keys in text-based chord charts and lead sheets.

For a list of apps and programs that take advantage of the four-pedal version of the AirTurn BT-105, visit http:// airturn.com/4-pedal-bt-105/apps/4-pedal-apps

The Toe Bone's Connected To The ...

As a pianist, I typically use my left foot to operate my AirTurn pedal for turning pages, since I don't use the Una corda – otherwise known as the "soft pedal" – nearly as frequently as my right foot on the damper pedal. "But what if you need to use a pedal and an AirTurn at the same time?" I frequently hear from Una corda addicts. Ah, dear pianist, here's a solution I gleaned from my days as an amateur organist:

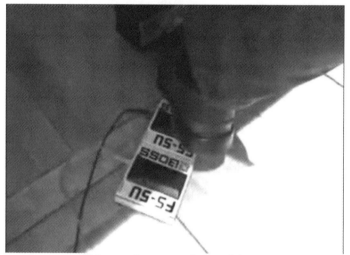

Using one foot to control two pedals at once

Organists playing on pedal keyboards learn a "heel-toe" technique. This same technique can be applied to press the Una corda pedal and an AirTurn pedal at the same time – just angle the AirTurn pedal accordingly, and within reach of your heel at an outturned angle. Any more whiners out there?

Look Ma! No Hands ... Or Feet!

In chapter 12, we met organist Bob Bell, who came up with a novel way to turn pages while both hands and both feet are occupied (harpists and drummers are also musicians who need to be multi-limb-dexterous). He borrowed a solution developed by skydivers who wanted to take pictures while hurtling through the air: a bite switch connected to an AirTurn.

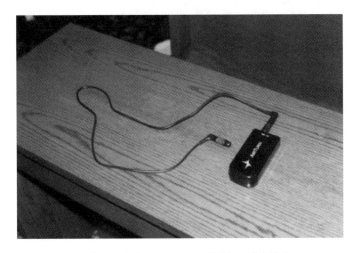

Bite switch connector an AirTurn AT-104

Organist Bob Bell demonstrates using a bite switch with and AirTurn to turn pages hands and feet free

Sleight of Palm: Pens for Tablets

As hard as Steve Jobs tried to kill the keyboard and the pen with the iPad, the fact remains that the humble pen still remains the tool of choice for drawing detailed annotations in music. The problem is that despite the cool innovations of "multi-touch" with the iPad's interface, if you want to use a pen or iPad-ready stylus, you still need to keep your palm off the screen in order to cleanly apply your ink markings. That makes for some pretty awkward John Hancocks that have to be implemented with a Chinese calligraphy brush style of penmanship.

The iPad's capacitive screen (along with other tablets that use the same capacitive technology) relies on a bioelectric current from the user's finger (shocking, isn't it?). What that bit of techno-mumbo-jumbo means is that the iPad screen isn't really designed for precision ink drawing. The result is a whole class of pens and styluses for the iPad that have to use a conductive foam or other squishy material in order to apply digital ink on screen. Needless to say, pens + iPads = a messy inking experience. With that in mind, here is a look at some of the top pens for the iPad:

Pogo Stylus by Ten One Design

The Pogo Stylus was one of the first iPad-friendly pens on the market. Its squishy foam tip feels weird applied on a glass screen, but it's marginally effective as a digital inker. The skinny body makes it easy to carry around (and easy to lose), and can get some getting used to.

Wacom Bamboo Stylus for the iPad

Wacom is famous for creating digital drawing slates for Mac and PC computers, as well as being the primary pen technology for Tablet PCs when they were still in production. TheVerge.com proclaims the Bamboo Stylus for the iPad as being one of the best available, due to its more comfortable grip and smaller (albeit still squishy) tip.

Jot Pro by Adonit

The Jot Pro is arguably the most accurate stylus for the iPad. Instead of a squishy foam or rubber tip, the Jot Pro uses a clear rotating disc that shows exactly where you are applying the pen tip as well as providing a stable writing surface. It even features a magnetic body that stays affixed to the newer iPads that utilize the magnetic covers.

Detail of the Jot Pro's Rotating Disc Tip

For fans of Android tablets (and tablets in general), the Samsung Galaxy Note series features the pen to beat. Users can rest their palms comfortably on the capacitive screen while drawing effortless scribbles with a digital pen that feels decadently luxurious.

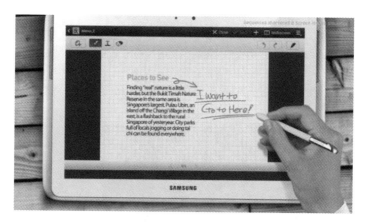

Samsung's Notable Pen for the Galaxy Tab

Microsoft Makes A Comeback

With the Surface Pro tablet, Microsoft is making a comeback of sorts. The older Tablet PCs featured Wacom-designed pens that worked marvelously. On screens with touch capabilities, the Wacom pens could still be applied with the palm resting comfortably against the screen, as the computer would recognize when the pen was being used and deactivate input from palms, fingers, and other human appendages (wipe that naughty thought from your brain, you monkey you!). The Surface Pro revives the intelligent pen that can be used naturally as a pen, instead of as a third hand.

Microsoft Surface Pro

Drawing Tablets for Mac and PC Computers

If you've eschewed diminutive tablets but still want to be able to draw ink markings comfortably on a larger laptop or Mac/PC computer screen, you'll want to consider a drawing tablet. Wacom is the undisputed leader in graphics tablets for computers, and their Bamboo line is a great place to start. The graphic tablet connects to your computer via a USB cable and operates like a mouse, but with the ergonomic bliss of an honest-to-goodness pen in your hand. It can take a little get used to drawing without your hand directly on the screen, but if you can use a mouse, then you'll take to a digitizer tablet pen in no time.

Wacom Bamboo Connect Graphics Tablet for Mac and PC

CHAPTER THIRTY-SIX

Conclusion: It's Never Too Late

David Kim, Concertmaster of The Philadelphia Orchestra, likes to share tales of his "DK" moments. Like the time his wife broke her ankle and begged him not to forget his music before leaving for a series of concerts in Japan, lest she have to schlep up and down the five flights of stairs in their home to scan and email his Brahms Violin Concerto part while taking care of their two daughters. Sure enough, despite his promises to the contrary, David forgot his part, and he had to contend with begging his wife to scan the music, email the part, and convince the Japanese staff with poor English skills to print and bind his music.

Or the time he was playing a recital in New Jersey and left his music in his dressing room, forcing him to yell out for the stage manager to unlock the door, much to the bemusement of the audience. Or the time he forgot his part to a Handel sonata and had to enlist his pianist to make an enlarged photocopy of the piano score, snip out the violin lines, and paste them like a jigsaw puzzle onto a huge piece of poster board, resulting in the delayed – and chagrined – start to his recital.

At the ripe old age of 49, and as leader of one of the world's most prestigious – and old-fashioned – symphony orchestras, David realized that he needed to take a serious look at a digital alternative to his paper-music woes. He invested in an iPad and with the help of his assistant started scanning his paper music into PDF files. But he had a host of concerns about making the transition from paper to pixels:

- Would it be too complicated to use?
- Would there be a mess of wires to contend with on stage?
- Would the page turning pedal make a clicking noise like a mouse, or turn too many pages at once accidentally?
- What if he forgot to bring his knapsack at the airport security line and left his iPad – and all his music – behind?
- What if he were stuck in a part of the world with no Internet connection?

Would it be too complicated to use?

David would be the first to admit that he – like the vast majority of musicians, particularly classical ones – is pretty technology challenged. Be that as it may, when David received his AirTurn BT-105, he turned it on, followed the instructions for going into his iPad's settings, tapped the AirTurn listing under the Bluetooth settings to pair them together – and that was it. Paired and done. One pedal to turn pages forwards, the other to turn pages backwards. Easy peasy.

Would there be a mess of wires to contend with on stage?

With the iPad's 10-hour battery life, David realized there was no need to keep it plugged in to an ugly extension cord on stage. And since the AirTurn BT-105 is equipped with a 100-hour rechargeable battery and connects wirelessly to the iPad with Bluetooth technology, no wires were needed for the page turner as well.

Would the page-turning pedal make a clicking noise like a mouse, or turn too many pages at once accidentally?

Thanks to the ATFS-2's mechanism-free design, there were no parts to click or squeak or make any noise whatsoever when pressed to activate a page turn with the BT-105. And with the BT-105's built-in debounce circuitry, that prevented multiple pages from being turned accidentally.

What if he forgot to bring his knapsack at the airport security line and left his iPad – and all his music – behind?

David realized that – thanks to the popularity of tablets like the iPad around the world – he could simply borrow someone else's iPad or MacBook computer to read his music. But what about his own music? Wouldn't it be stuck in his personal iPad? Well, thanks to technologies like Dropbox, David realized that he could keep a copy of all his music online and access it through any internet-ready device. The digital nature of his music meant that it could be stored and accessed anywhere in the world, and not stuck in any given physical location like paper music.

What if he were stuck in a part of the world with no Internet connection?

It's pretty hard to find a place in the world these days that doesn't have Internet access. Anywhere you can find a McDonald's or a Starbucks store, you can take advantage of their Internet services. And just about every university worldwide provides wireless Internet access. Ditto for hotels nowadays.

As David checked off his reservations one by one, he began to discover that going digital is – in his own words – "dummy-proof."

And if David can make the transition from paper to pixels and actually get excited about it, so can you.

For a video series of David Kim talking about his digital sheet music setup and tutorials for using his equipment, visit http://airturn.com/classical-music/solutions/classical-music

Appendix A:
How to Create Big-Note Versions of Sheet Music for
the iPad Using a Mac

The number-one complaint about using an iPad to read digital sheet music is the diminutive size of its 9.7-inch screen. For musicians with relatively normal eyesight, that's already a slight compromise adjusting from paper pages that are at least 8.5″ x 11″ or larger. One way to compensate for the visual contraction is to use an app that can display the music a half-page at a time when you turn the iPad sideways ("landscape mode," for you geeks out there). That at least brings the size of the music on par with a regular sheet of paper, albeit a half-page at a time.

Reading sheet music on an upright iPad ("portrait mode")

Viewing music a half-page at a time with the iPad rotated sideways ("landscape mode") – note the larger view of the music notes compared to the upright view.

But what if you are a musician with aging eyes, or suffering from a low-vision condition like macular degeneration, or something even worse like Retinitis pigmentosa (RP) where your field of vision is reduced to a small tunnel? In the physical world, your best solution would be to run to a Kinko's and get your music copied at a high-enough zoom level to blow up your notes to a legible level onto the largest paper size available. In the digital world, you could resort to using a ginormous display, but that isn't practical if you happen to be a musician that needs to be anything more mobile than an organist.

Recently, during a long drive home from taking my oldest boy to college, the mother of a 14-year-old music student called me to see if anything could be done to help her daughter suffering from RP. She wanted to be able to participate in band camp, but was frustrated with having to carry around huge stacks of oversized paper music with zoomed copies of her music. She loved the idea of putting her entire sheet-music library into a svelte iPad and then turning digital pages hands free with a device like an <u>AirTurn</u>, but the half-page view for most apps was still too small for her vision condition. Was there any way to zoom her music even larger, say, to be able to just see one or two measures at a time?

The bad news was, barring the use of an external larger monitor, there was no way for any iPad app to natively display sheet music larger than the geometric boundaries of the page and still enable a practical page-turning solution beyond manually pinching and zooming the page. That would mean keeping two fingers constantly pincer-glued to the screen – not very practical for an instrumental musician who needs two hands to play her instrument.

The good news was, we were working with *digital* sheet music (the band director had been thoughtful enough to provide PDF versions of the sheet music), which meant that with enough creativity and imagination, we could find a way to refashion the page to suit her needs. I asked the mother what type of computer they owned, and she told me that they had a Mac. I asked her to open one of the PDF files on her Mac and set the view to maximize the width of the page:

I then asked her to press a three-key combination on her Mac keyboard:

Command (⌘) + Shift + 4

This brought up a small reticule, enabling her to use her mouse to click and hold the mouse button while dragging a rectangle around two measures of music at a time.

Releasing the button would create an image file on her desktop containing the screen snippet she had just selected.

335

This screenshot file would be titled "Screen Shot" with the full date (year, month, day) and time (hour, minute, second) that the screen was created.

Going a few measures at a time and creating this collection of screen shots, she would then gather them into another fantastic free program called iCombiner, which works to combine multiple-image and document files into a single PDF file. Since all the files were time stamped, she needed to make sure that she used the "date modified" header within her file-navigation window to set all the files in the correct order, with the oldest on top and newest on the bottom, before clicking the top file, then shift-clicking the bottom file (to select all the files in a group), then dragging the whole set into the iCombiner file window.

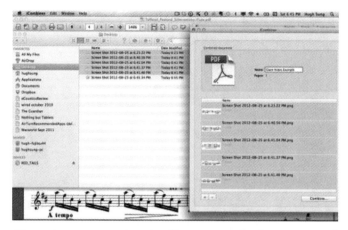

Once she was sure that the files were set in the correct order, she could give the PDF file a name and then press the "Combine" button – and voila! She now had a PDF eBook with each page showing ginormous views of her music a few measures at a time (she could even select just one measure at a time if necessary).

The next step was to transfer her PDF file into an app that would provide an optimal view of these custom-cut pages. It turns out that DeepDish Gigbook does the best job of displaying these pages, with a nice centered alignment in the middle of the screen and a dark background to help isolate the view. Here's what the music looks like within DeepDish Gigbook on an iPad:

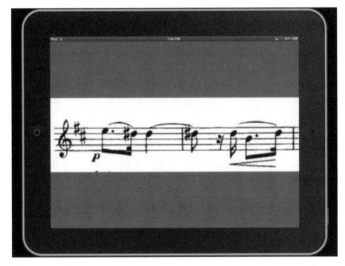

So, with the sun setting on a beautiful Pennsylvania countryside and the wind whistling through my SUV window, this digital cowboy closed his cell phone and drove home contented that his pixel-rustling skills were up to the challenge to help another musician in distress. In our next appendix, we'll detail how to make a giant-note version of sheet music with a Windows PC.

Appendix B:
How to Create Big-Note Versions of Sheet Music for the iPad Using a PC

This is really hard for me to admit as a longtime die-hard Windows user, but I really enjoy the smooth workflow of creating custom screen clips on my Mac. I wanted to see if I could come as close as possible to recreating that workflow with my Windows PC to make the tedious task of creating big-note versions of digital sheet-music scores a little less so.

Windows 7 and Windows Vista operating systems come bundled with a handy little program called Snipping Tool – just do a search for it from the "Start" button.

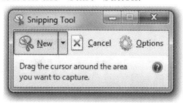

Snipping Tool gives you the option to create rectangular or freehand selections of the screen and save them as image files and even mark them up with ink and highlight annotations. The only problem with Snipping Tools is that it requires you to move your mouse around to select the tool, activate a new snip, name the file, etc. ... all the mousing around can make it easy to lose your place on the digital page when you have to scan dozens of cuts per page. I would rather use as few mouse movements and keyboard taps as possible to keep my workflow streamlined.

Gadwin PrintScreen is a great alternative to Snipping Tool – it's free, and it's available for all versions of Windows, including ol' faithful Windows XP. You can assign a hotkey (geek talk for a specific key on your keyboard to activate the program – the default for Gadwin PrintScreen is the "PrtSc"/PrintScreen button) and a host of other custom features. Here's a walkthrough of my recommended setup:

339

After you install Gadwin PrintScreen, you should see its icon appear in your taskbar:

Right click on the icon to bring up its menu options, and select **"Properties."**

Along the left-hand column, click on "Source." In the main window to the right, within the "Captured area" pane, select the radio button for "Rectangular Area."

Next, select the "Image" option in the left column. In the main window under "Type of Image," you will see that the default file format is Windows Bitmap (*.bmp). Click on the drop-down menu and select JPEG Bitmat (*.jpg) instead.

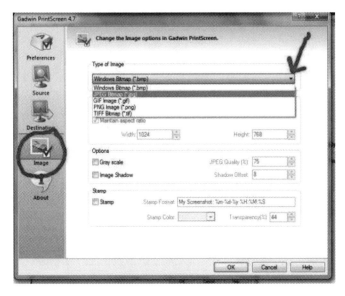

Click the "OK" button on the bottom and your preferences will be saved.

Next, we will want to install a virtual PDF printer to convert your clipped-image files into PDF files. One of my favorites is a free program called doPDF, which you can download from http://www.dopdf.com/

After you download and install doPDF, you're ready to go.

Open up your sheet-music PDF file with a PDF reader like Adobe Reader and set the view to maximize the width of the page you want to work with.

If you are using Gadwin PrintScreen's default hotkey setup, press the PrtSc key and you should see a magnification reticle appear:

Click your left mouse button and drag a rectangle around the measures you want to clip.

Press "Enter" and your selection will appear in a popup window.

Press "Enter" again and you will see a confirmation popup saying that the capture has been completed. Hit "Enter" again to make the popup disappear.

Go back and repeat for all the successive measures you want to clip on the screen. Once you're done, navigate to your **Documents** folder, then look for the **PrintScreen Files** folder. You will see all your screen clips automatically named as ScreenShot### where the ### will automatically increment the order that the clips were created.

Press the key combination Ctrl+A to select all the files within the PrintScreen Files folder, and then click on "Print" in the folder menu bar.

In the "Print Pictures" window, make sure you select "doPDF v7" as the printer in the top left menu bar. If you notice that the image in the preview window is oriented the wrong way, then you will need to adjust the paper settings. Click on "Options" in the lower right corner.

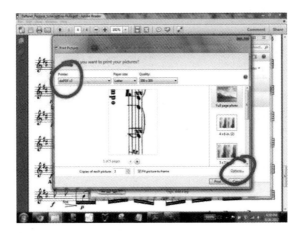

In the next popup window, click on the "Printer Properties" link.

In the next screen within the "Orientation" panel on the lower right, make sure that the "landscape" radio button is selected, then click "OK."

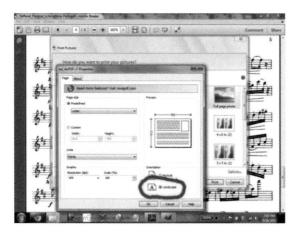

Now the preview window will show the screen clip in the proper orientation, but the zoom may be incorrect. Make sure that the "Fit picture to frame" box is unselected (click on it to remove the check mark).

Click on "Print," and you will see a dialogue box pop up, giving you the option to name the PDF file within the "File name" box. Just change the text after "C:\Users\Your Name \Documents\" and make sure you leave the ".pdf" after your file name. In this example, I changed the file name to "Giant Note PC Example.pdf." Click on "OK" to create the PDF file.

You will find your new file within your "Documents" folder. Use iTunes to connect to your iPad and transfer the file into the DeepDish Gigbook app file window (see the section on "Transferring Converted Music to an iPad using iTunes"). Here's how the final PDF giant-note sheet-music page looks with the iPad turned to its side:

Appendix C: Big-Note Beta

Creating custom versions of PDF sheet music to accommodate low-vision needs on small-tablet screens is a "good news/bad news" proposition. The good news is – as we've seen in the previous two appendices – that it's possible. The bad news is that the process for doing so is admittedly tedious and time consuming. Multiply this with a sizeable library, and the proverbial elephant on your dinner plate just became the hors d'oeuvres for a much larger gastro-nightmare.

Quite literally a few days before the completion of this book, I proposed an idea to Marco Leoné, the developer of MusicReader PDF 4, a PDF-reading program for Mac and PC computers tailored to the specific needs of musicians. What if there were a way to come up with a program that could automatically resize the view of a static PDF-sheet of music to show only a few measures at a time to maximize the real estate of a smaller screen?

Marco pointed out that an earlier version of MusicReader (MusicReader 3) had automatic measure detection built in, so he set about putting together a beta program for applying that technology to a special utility for reformatting PDF sheet music so that each page would only show the number of measures a user desires. Here's the result of a preliminary test:

Original Score:

Music engraving by LilyPond 2.16.1—www.lilypond.org

Resulting score resized to show only three measures at a time:

Note how the program was able to splice the last measure of the first line into the beginning of the next line seamlessly, and how the remaining lines get automatically split and reconnected accordingly. Not only will this work with single-line music, but the program can recognize multiple staves and work accordingly. You will also be able to isolate and extract individual parts from a combined score. Pretty nifty, eh?

Now, keep in mind that the accuracy of the measure detection will depend on the "cleanliness" of the PDF file. You'll need to make sure your scans are showing the staff lines as straight as possible (PDFs made from digital music notation software are ideal, as opposed to image scans of paper-printed music). If the program gets wonky with its measure detection, you'll have the option to manually designate the proper layout.

Again, this is the very earliest beta at the time of this writing, but hopefully by the time I get around to writing the next edition of this book, the program will be up and running and available to the public. To sign up for updates, visit http://largeprintmusic.com/

Ain't technology grand?

Appendix C: Big-Note Beta

Appendix D:
A Digital Musician's Pre-Performance Checklist

One summer, I was invited to be on the faculty of the Rocky Ridge Music Center. Being situated in the beautiful Colorado Rockies, I thought it was a great opportunity to bring my family along with me and sign up my boys for a session at the YMCA camp while I was working. One particularly hectic day, I was scheduled to accompany some students for a noontime recital immediately after a full morning of teaching lessons. I didn't have time to drive my boys to camp, so I asked one of the counselors to take my rental car and drop them off. Just as the recital was about to begin, I realized to my horror that I had left my tablet PC in the car – the one that I was using to read the music for the performance!

I had a backup laptop and only five minutes to get ready

before I was supposed to take the stage with the young violinist. I feverishly logged on to IMSLP.org and downloaded a copy of the concerto she was supposed to play. Just as the PDF finished downloading, it was our turn to perform. I propped the laptop on the piano, and the performance began. The poor violinist was terribly nervous, and I did my best to maintain a supportive tempo for her.

Suddenly, my worst fears came true. Just as we were in the thick of the piece, the screen on my laptop blacked out and the music winked into oblivion, bringing the performance to a screeching halt and the frayed nerves of the violinist to a melting point. What an idiot – in my rush to set up a computer that wasn't prepared for use in musical performance, I neglected my typical pre-performance checklist to make sure the power-saving features of my laptop were deactivated. In essence, my laptop went to sleep to save battery power.

Many of my musical colleagues point out their fear that something like this would go wrong if they ever decided to make the transition to digital sheet music. What if the computer crashes in the middle of a performance? What if the screen freezes right before a critical page turn? So on and so forth. But I need to emphasize that in my thousands of performances using digital sheet music, I can count on half a hand the number of times my digital set up failed me, and each failure had a clear cause due to rushed preparation ahead of time, never a system failure with the computer itself. In other words, good ol' fashioned human error.

Computers nowadays are much, much more reliable than their counterparts in the past, and as long as you aren't rendering Hi-Def video files while cavorting around in World of Warcraft or multi-chatting with Facebook friends during tacets, your computer will be more than up to the task of displaying music reliably. Compared to my absent-minded handling of paper music (misplacing music, forgetting to bring scores, etc.) coupled with the nightmare of dealing with incompetent human page turners, my paper failure rate was much, much higher than my digital one. Nowadays, I actually feel safer with my iPad sitting on my piano rack than with a wobbly piece of paper music that might have pages stuck together due to humidity on stage, or binding that's too stiff to keep the pages open, making them susceptible to being blown over by an errant draft.

Just as a guitar player makes sure he has extra strings in his case or a clarinet player has the right pieces of cane prepared for her reeds, a digital musician will want to approach their music reading computer with the same level of care and understanding as their own instruments. Here is my pre-performance checklist for digital sheet music, broken down in three stages:

1.   Preparation (setting up your computer as a performance tool ahead of time)

2.   Pre-Concert (usually the night before show time)

3.   Pre-Performance (last-minute checks before walking on stage)

1. Preparation

-          Make sure your power-saving settings are set to "off" or "never."

-          Turn off any screen savers, or at least set them to a time limit that begins well beyond the length of your performance.

-          Check your computer for anti-virus or auto-update settings (Windows computers are notorious for rebooting for updates when you least expect them to). Set notification messages to "off" or "hidden," and make sure your update settings are set to "manual" instead of "automatic" (leaving it up to you to manually reboot your computer for updates, rather than your operating system).

-          Make sure you have all the music you need in your computer from scanned, downloaded or purchased sources.

-          Run through all the pages to make sure nothing is missing or illegible, and adjust for repeats or Da capos as necessary (I once discovered in the middle of a lesson that the last page of the Bruch Violin Concerto No. 2 that I had transferred from a CD sheet music collection was missing. What a gyp!).

- If you are using backing tracks, make sure you have all the audio files you need and that they are properly linked to your sheet music as needed.

2. Pre-Concert

- Make sure your computer's batteries are fully charged.

- If you are using an accessory like the AirTurn Bluetooth page-turning pedal, make sure that it's charged as needed.

- Go through any set lists you have created and make sure all the pages are turning properly and that all songs are opening in the proper order

- Turn off any alarm, calendar, or instant message notification settings. Last thing you want in the middle of a performance is an alarm popping open in front of your music reminding you to pick up snacks for poker night!

3. Pre-Performance

- Close all programs/apps except for the one(s) you need for reading your music and/or playing your backing tracks.

- On computers, pay particular attention to apps that run in the background, like instant-messaging programs, Skype, anti-virus programs, and the like. Make sure they are completely closed for the duration of the gig.

- On the iPad, double click the home button to bring up a row of app icons on the bottom of the screen representing all the apps that are open and active. Press and hold any app icon until all the icons wiggle and a small red minus sign appears on the upper left of each app icon. Tap the minus signs to close the apps.

iPad apps ready to be closed

- On Android tablets, download a free app called <u>Advanced Task Killer</u>. Run it to close all active apps, then open only the app(s) you need for the performance.

- Make sure the screen brightness is set to your liking. Keep in mind that if you are relying on battery power for really long gigs, you may want to dim the screen to 50% brightness in order to conserve battery and prevent a mid-gig tablet nap.

- If you are controlling multiple slave tablets from a master tablet, make sure that all tablets are properly connected and sending/receiving signals for turning pages or opening songs in set lists.

- If you aren't controlling multiple tablets, turn WiFi off.

- If you are using a page-turning accessory like the AirTurn, make sure the pages are turning correctly. For the BT-105, make sure the Bluetooth setting on the host computer is turned on and receiving signals properly.

Once you've taken the time and foresight to go through your checklist, all that's left to do is say "Toi Toi" (the rough equivalent of "break a leg" in Opera-speak), hit the stage, and have a magical performance!

Acknowledgments

I want to thank my colleagues – faculty, staff, and students – of The Curtis Institute of Music for giving me the best MBA training during my 19 years there, and for giving me the perfect laboratory to experiment with all my crazy digital sheet-music contraptions, wonky page-turning pedals, and social-data management through my developments of the first database-driven recital/gig/accompanist time-sheet system in existence at any major music conservatory. I want to particularly thank Bob Fitzpatrick, Dean-extraordinaire at Curtis until 2009 for sitting me in his office one day and asking me point-blank, "Why are you still here?" His send-off letter at my Curtis tea-time "farewell ceremony" was one of the most touching tributes ever.

I want to extend a special thanks to my "Camelot team" at AirTurn – to Lester, my mentor, business-guru, and all-around vegan and life counselor for opening my eyes to the "art" of business; to Karna, for her infectious positivity and always flashing a winning smile even under the most strenuous of circumstances; to Matt, for all his attention to the fine details and for keeping the engine running smoothly; and to Ginny, for her love and incredible passion for all the ways we're trying to make the world a better place through the endeavors of our amazing little company.

Thank you to Dave Elderkin, Carol Hauptfuhrer, and Henry Karplus - true angels who put their faith in our company and cheered us on as we grew.

Special thanks to James Townsend, my hyphen-happy super-human editor for making this book SO much more interesting and side-splittingly funny; to Lori and her pedagogy class for giving me the inspiration for the outline of this book; to SoYoung for being the crazy woman that met me backstage after that fateful recital and introducing me to Lester; to Melissa for carving out an incredible oasis for writing with inspiration; to Bill Gates for coming up with the idea of the Tablet PC and turning on all the light bulbs in my head; to the late Steve Jobs for getting the rest of the world to catch up to Bill's ideas; to Tony Bennett for blocking out the annoying developer trying to pitch his business idea to the investor next to him in that plane ride and giving me the perfect voice for this book; to Jungeun for being the best boss in the world when the tables turned and I stopped being her boss; to Hilary and her wonderful father, for putting up with me so graciously as I left my music behind while jet-setting across the country on tour; to Aaron, for chomping on his cigar and scaring me silly with the limitations of out-of-print paper music, as well as teaching me to use "the force" to truly listen to what makes music work; to David for reminding me that while business people are a dime-a-dozen, true musicians are priceless; to Mrs. Sokoloff for giving me fingers of steel, Mr. Bolet for teaching me to make art outside of the box, and to Mr. Lipkin for teaching me to analyze said box nonetheless; to Pat and the wonderful Masterworks family for making me feel like the "world's greatest pianist" [sic]; to Da-Hong for reminding me that tech without talent and hard work is meaningless; and to my beloved family for putting up with my workaholic obsessions with grace, patience, rolled eyes, and lots of love. Paul, Eric, and Timmy, my hope is that you will grow up to find your passions that make the world a better place. I love you dearly and am so very, very proud of each of you.

About the Author

Classical pianist Hugh Sung has been dreaming about finding cool ways to integrate his love of music and technology ever since his childhood days glued to TV episodes of Star Trek, The Six Million Dollar Man, and countless viewings of all the original Star Wars movies. Hugh's musical career has seen him perform all over the world, including recitals at Carnegie's Weill Hall and Issac Stern Auditorium, the National Gallery of Art, and most recently at Wallenstein Castle in Prague, Czech Republic. As a collaborative pianist, he has worked with the likes of violinists Hilary Hahn, Leila Josefowicz, and Aaron Rosand; flutists Julius Baker, Jeffrey Khaner, and Gary Schocker; composers Jennifer Higdon, Richard Danielpour, and Daron Hagen, among many others. His recordings for the Biddulph, Avie, Vox, Azica, I Virtuosi, and CRI labels can be found on iTunes, Amazon MP3, and other major online distributors. When Microsoft came out with its first Tablet PC's in 2002, Hugh realized that this was the device that could solve all of his vexing problems with paper music scores. He became an early adopter of digital music scores and now works completely paper-free in all his rehearsals, lessons, performances and recording sessions.Before co-founding AirTurn with Lester Karplus, Hugh was a collaborative piano faculty member at the Curtis Institute of Music, having previously served as its Director of Student Recitals and Instrumental Accompaniment.

Visit the companion website to this book at www.frompapertopixels.com

For the latest updates in the world of digital sheet music, visit www.facebook.com/airturn